A Historic Point of Departure: Bringing the Israeli-Palestinian Conflict to a Close and Creating a New Regional Geopolitical Order

A HISTORIC
POINT OF DEPARTURE

*Bringing the Israeli-Palestinian Conflict to a Close and
Creating a New Regional Geopolitical Order*

ALON BEN-MEIR

Westphalia Press
An Imprint of the Policy Studies Organization
Washington, DC
2024

Westphalia Press
An imprint of Policy Studies Organization
1367 Connecticut Avenue NW
Washington, D.C. 20036
info@ipsonet.org

ISBN: 978-1-63723-640-6

Cover and interior design by Jeffrey Barnes
jbarnesbook.design

Daniel Gutierrez-Sandoval, Executive Director
PSO and Westphalia Press

Updated material and comments on this edition
can be found at the Westphalia Press website:
www.westphaliapress.org

DEDICATION

I dedicate this book to all families suffering from the loss of their loved ones throughout the century-old Israeli-Palestinian conflict, especially those who died during the unfathomable terrorist attack on Israel on October 7, 2023, and those who continue to die as we witness the unfolding horror in Gaza. Every one of us should spare no effort to help bring closure to this tragic conflict and save the lives of countless innocent men, women, and children on both sides who need not die in vain.

TABLE OF CONTENTS

INTRODUCTION

Hamas' savage attack and Israel's massive retaliation have shaken the dynamic of the Israeli-Palestinian conflict to the core, making it impossible to return to the status quo that existed before October 7. An Israeli-Palestinian peace based on a two-state solution has come back to the fore, and it is now considered by major regional and international players as the only viable option that will bring closure to their 76-year-old conflict. What it would take now is to translate statements made in support of a two-state solution, especially by the US and the Arab states, into action by offering a comprehensive framework for peace initiated by the US and Saudi Arabia and co-sponsored by Egypt and Jordan, and *addressed directly to the Israeli and Palestinian publics.* Such a framework could usher in a new era shaped by novel alliances, *creating a crescent extending from the Gulf states to the Mediterranean*, preceded by an Israeli-Palestinian peace agreement based on a two-state solution—a prerequisite necessary for establishing such an alliance. *Every country in the region seeks such an outcome* under the US security umbrella. This will decisively improve their geostrategic position while bolstering their security and diminishing any outside threat, leading to unprecedented prosperity and growth.

Although some will say that I am overly optimistic, I maintain that the elements for a breakthrough of such a historic magnitude, though created by tragic events, *do exist.* It will take, however, courageous, visionary, and committed leadership on all sides to act, which are not deterred by undue political consideration and the many intractable issues that lay ahead to reach a peace agreement that has eluded many US, Arab, Israeli, and Palestinian governments in the past.

President Biden, along with Saudi Arabia's Crown Prince Mohammed bin Salman, Jordan's King Abdullah, and Egypt's President Sisi, has an opportunity to engage in a historic point of departure from the traditional US approach to the Israeli-Palestinian conflict.

The question is, will they seize this opportunity that presented itself following Hamas' attack and Israel's retaliation that makes it impossible to return to the status quo ante, and bring a closure to the Israeli-Palestinian conflict?

BACKGROUND

On October 6, 2023, I flew from Tel Aviv, Israel, to Amman, Jordan. On October 7, Hamas attacked, which sent a shock wave throughout the region even before a full assessment of the scope of the attack and its horrific consequences became known. While still in Amman on October 9, I published the following piece, which remains extremely relevant to the peace proposal I am advancing in this book. Due to its relevance, I am using it verbatim as the background because it illuminates the essence of the Israeli-Palestinian conflict and raises the question: *Where do we go from here?*

HAMAS' BRUTAL ATTACK COULD HAVE BEEN AVOIDED

AMMAN – October 9, 2023

I certainly join the voices of many leaders who condemned Hamas' attack in the strongest terms. That said, I am not as surprised as many that this attack has, in fact, taken place and claimed the lives of so many innocent Israelis, nor will I be surprised by the ongoing Israeli retaliation that will certainly claim the lives of hundreds if not thousands of Palestinians, including many innocent civilians. I'm not surprised because, like many of us who have been following the development of events between Israel and the Palestinians in the last few years, especially the past several months, I easily came to the conclusion—and stated a number of times in my writing—that it was only a question of when such a flare-up would take place.

I wrote the following paragraph just over a year ago (originally published on October 2, 2022), which has tragically come to pass in the last couple of days.

> The danger that all concerned parties seem to overlook is that although on the surface, the status quo between Israel and the Palestinians may prevail for a little longer, say three to four years,

it cannot be sustained for much beyond that. It is bound to explode in the face of everyone who does not realize the urgency and the dire consequences in the absence of a solution. Indeed, it is not a matter of *if* but *when* the Palestinians will rise and resort to violence, making the Second Intifada in 2000 look like a mere rehearsal. And the Israelis who have been living in denial will sooner rather than later have to face the bitter truth. The Palestinian problem will not go away; it will continue to haunt them and offer no respite. Moreover, the conflict with the Palestinians will continue to provide Israel's staunchest enemy, Iran, and its proxy Hezbollah in Lebanon, the perfect recipe they need to destabilize the region and constantly threaten Israel's national security. And whereas Israel can prevail militarily over any of its enemies, albeit at an increasing toll in blood and treasure, it cannot stop the most dangerous threat of all—the deadly erosion, resulting from its continuing brutal occupation, of that moral foundation on which the country was established.[i]

This unprecedented and unimaginable attack by Hamas, from the land, air, and sea, must have taken months to plan, train, and prepare for execution. And yet Israel's 'most sophisticated' intelligence agencies did not detect even a hint of such a devastating plan. What does that say about the Israeli government, led by an arrogant and self-conceited prime minister, Netanyahu, who brags about Israel's unmatched military capabilities and preparedness?

While Netanyahu was busy plotting to crush Israel's democracy through his so-called judicial reforms, and reinforcing Israel's security in the West Bank by sending thousands of troops to protect the settlers who have been rampaging against the Palestinians, Hamas was preparing for this deadly attack on an unprecedented scale, claiming the lives of, as of this writing, 700 Israelis and abducting over 100,[1] while exposing Israel's vulnerability in the eyes of its strongest enemies—including Hezbollah and Iran.

The timing of Hamas' attack obviously was not accidental. It was planned to take place exactly on the 50th anniversary of the 1973 Yom Kippur War. It was meant to crudely remind the Israelis that the Palestinians' rights and aspirations are not a box to be checked off, as Netanyahu recently described when asked about the prospective normalization of relations between Israel and Saudi Arabia.

No Israeli could have possibly believed that a so-called "ragtag group" with "firecrackers," as some Israeli officials have described Hamas, which has been under blockade for eighteen years, would be in a position to mount an attack of such magnitude, sending tens of thousands of Israelis to shelters, cowering in fear. For decades, the Israeli government has led the public to believe that the Palestinians will not cease their fight for independence unless Israel enacts brutal force against them. This attack has proven that claim false; that even under the harshest circumstances the Palestinians will never give up their fight for freedom and independence by answering violence with violence—and will never succumb to Israeli forces.

The current Israeli government, whose minister in charge of civilian affairs in the West Bank, Bezalel Smotrich, called earlier this year for wiping out the Palestinian village of Huwara[2] and has given free rein to settlers to harass Palestinians at every turn, did nothing but usurp the last vestiges of hope for the Palestinians to be free again. To treat the Palestinians as if they are the occupier rather than being occupied, as Smotrich has claimed, is not only outra-

---

1   The updated numbers, after the immediate aftermath of the attack, are generally accepted as approximately 1,200 killed and 240 taken as hostages.

2   See Rami Ayyub, "Israeli Minister's Call to 'erase' Palestinian Village an Incitement to Violence, US Says," Reuters, March 1, 2023, https://www.reuters.com/world/middle-east/israeli-ministers-call-erase-palestinian-village-an-incitement-violence-us-says-2023-03-01/.

geous but self-defeating, as has been proven over the last 75 years. For Saturday's brutal attack by Hamas to occur under the watch of the most militant government in Israel's history has only proven its ineptitude; ignoring the Palestinian problem will be at Israel's peril.

Hamas knew too well that the people of Gaza would suffer massive losses of life and destruction for attacking Israel on such an unprecedented scale. The extent of the casualties and destruction inflicted by Israel already attests to that. They have nevertheless taken such a deadly but calculated risk because they were determined to change the dynamic of the conflict with Israel, create a new paradigm, and force Israel to reevaluate its position toward the Palestinians. I found it interesting that Hamas' spokesperson didn't call for Israel's destruction but rather called for an end to violations against Palestinians, stating, "We want the international community to stop atrocities in Gaza, against Palestinian people, our holy sites like Al-Aqsa. All these things are the reason behind starting this battle."[ii] This is in response to the provocateur Itamar Ben-Gvir, who since he assumed the position of National Security Minister, has deliberately visited the Temple Mount to pray, which is in violation of a 1967 agreement between Jordan and Israel.

Whereas Hamas' militant wing, the Al-Qassam Brigades, has never reconciled itself with Israel's existence and *must be destroyed*, Israel should send a clear message that it is willing to initiate peace negotiations with moderate Palestinian leaders to create a long-term reconciliation process that will lead to a permanent solution. It is time for Israel to realize that the policy of going to Gaza to "mow the lawn" every few years has failed miserably and accomplished nothing but deepen their resistance. The recent horrifying attack attests to this perilously misguided Israeli policy.

Although Israel has every right to defend itself and crush the irredeemable Hamas and Islamic Jihad terrorists, who are backed by Iran and Hezbollah and will not accept Israel's reality, Israel must also remember that the vast majority of the Palestinian people want to live in peace, and accept Israel's right to exist. Sadly though, extremist governments such as the current one led by Netanyahu, portray the Palestinians as if they were all terrorists and can never be trusted; hence, they must be handled with an iron fist.

For how many more decades will Israel hold to this baseless, perilous, and counterproductive notion before it realizes the Palestinians are vastly ordinary people who want to live a normal life, just like any Israeli? They should remember that hopelessness breeds despair, and despair breeds anger and resentment, which in turn leaves the Palestinian people feeling no choice but to resort to violence and risk death rather than live a life of endless servitude and despair.

This reminds me of the absurd position of those Republicans who oppose gun control in the United States in the aftermath of mass shootings. After such an occurrence, they settle for sending prayers and condolences to the bereaved families, insisting that 'this is not the time' to talk about significant gun control laws, as if their prayers and condolences would stop the next mass shooting. But this obviously was never the case, as mass shootings and other gun violence continue, claiming the lives of nearly 50,000 Americans each year,[iii] and no effective gun control has been enacted. So is the case with any new ceasefire between Israel and Hamas, or Israel and the Palestinians. No ceasefire or condemnations will stop the conflict between the two sides. Those who are seeking peace, stability, security, and prosperity in the Middle East should remember that if Israeli-Saudi normalization is established and it does not incorporate a clear path for a solution to the Israeli-Palestinian conflict, it is nothing but a recipe for increasing regional violence and destabilization far beyond what we have seen thus far.

It is time for the Biden administration, which has been paying merely lip service to the two-state solution like all of its predecessors, to act on its formal position and insist that now is the time for Israel to take this conflict with the Palestinians seriously. The Biden administration must not assume for a moment that another ceasefire, regardless of its scope and length, will provide a lasting solution. Moreover, the Saudis must make it publicly clear that there will be no normalization of relations with Israel unless a clear path is established that would lead to a permanent solution to the Israeli-Palestinian conflict. Saying so publicly will allay the Palestinians' concerns that they will not be left behind to fend for themselves, while sending a clear message to the Israeli public that a solution to the Israeli-Palestinian conflict must be part and parcel of any agreement between Israel and Saudi Arabia, consistent with the 2002 Arab Peace Initiative. In the final analysis, it is only when the Israeli public demands *en masse* a new peace initiative will any Israeli government act in earnest toward that end.

Indeed, it is not enough for the Israelis to unite in times of crisis. They must now unite to demand a solution to the Israeli-Palestinian conflict. They must now pour into the streets by the hundreds of thousands, akin to their protests against Netanyahu's sinister effort to reform the judiciary, and remain relentless until their government agrees to enter into credible negotiations with the Palestinians. Failing to do so is to simply be waiting, once again, for the next horrifying conflagration that may even be more severe than this attack, and cause incalculable losses of life that no Israeli could imagine in their wildest nightmare.

Once the horrifying war has come to an end, and some sort of ceasefire takes place, tragically after thousands have been killed on both sides, a commission of inquiry should be set up to investigate how the Netanyahu government was caught off-guard. There is no doubt that this government has taken the relatively passive resistance of the Palestinians for granted, and never contemplated that they would ever be in a position to wage such an unprecedented assault. Those who are responsible in the government will have to be held accountable and pay the price.

Furthermore, the opposition leaders, Benny Gantz, Yair Lapid, Avigdor Lieberman, and Merav Michaeli, should heed Netanyahu's call for a unity government on the condition that once the war ends, he should resign and new elections be held.

Short of that, the Israeli public must demand the immediate resignation of Prime Minister Netanyahu. Instead of attending to Israel's national security needs, he has been busy plotting to severely undermine the judiciary and sacrifice the national interest only to save his own skin. He has betrayed the oath of his office and must now vacate it to restore dignity and confidence to the title he undeservedly carries.

* * * * *

To fully digest the complexities of the Israeli-Palestinian conflict and why a solution was not found over more than seven decades, it is extremely important to understand the psychological impediments that have and continue to haunt both sides. These impediments continue to prevent them from appreciating each other's legitimate concerns, anxieties, traumas, and fear—the mitigation of which is central to finding a solution the current outburst of violence has ironically provided.

PSYCHOLOGICAL IMPEDIMENTS ARE AT THE CORE OF THE ISRAELI-PALESTINIAN CONFLICT

The most puzzling aspect of the Israeli-Palestinian conflict is that after 76 years of mutual violence, enmity, and suffering, it remains unresolved even when coexistence is inevitable and a two-state solution remains the only viable option. Although many contentious issues must be specifically addressed and resolved before a final agreement can be implemented, especially the dispute over the land, it is the psychological dimension of the conflict that directly impacts every conflicting issue and makes it increasingly intractable. To mitigate the conflict, we must first look into the elements that inform the psychological dimension—psychological resistance, historical experience and perception, entrenched ideologies, mutual delegitimization, and religious conviction—and how to alleviate them as prerequisites to finding a solution.

The lack of any new significant development in recent years in the Israeli-Palestinian conflict is primarily attributed to the prevailing notion that neither side is able or willing, at least not at this juncture, to make any move toward solving their conflict. Both Israel and the Palestinians have been unable to articulate any realistic solution due to a lack of consensus between the Palestinian Authority and Hamas on one side, and within successive Israeli coalition governments on the other. Moreover, there is a robust segment of the Israeli population that objects in principle to the establishment of an independent Palestinian state and conversely, there is a strong constituency of Palestinian extremists led by Hamas who oppose the existence of Israel altogether. The past year has been intensely punctuated with violence, which has only served to highlight the stagnation in peace talks. For the past two decades, the conflict with the Palestinians became marginal at best and the idea of a two-state solution became almost taboo. The Israeli coalition government headed by Naftali Bennett and Yair Lapid that preceded the current Netanyahu-led one, made it an explicit part of their coalition agreement *to not address the Israeli-Palestinian conflict,* pushing it down the road for a future government to discuss as if it was an issue of no urgency and had no serious implication on Israel's future.[iv]

Despite the Israeli government's unwillingness to reach out to the Palestinians at this juncture, there is still a general consensus among many Israelis and Palestinians that the two-state solution remains the only viable one. Given however the adversarial relationship between the two sides for decades, it will be necessary to engage in a comprehensive reconciliation process for several years to pave the road for a direct peace negotiation to reach a peace agreement. The most critical part of such a process is mitigating the psychological dimension of the conflict in all its facets, as elaborated below.

Realities Drowned by Misconceptions

Generally, the Israeli-Palestinian conflict is viewed from the prism of a territorial dispute over the land stretching from the Mediterranean Sea to the Jordan River (the land of Israel/Palestine), in which both people have strong historical and religious roots. Whereas resolving the dispute over the land is critical to finding a solution, addressing the "intangible impediments" is a critical prerequisite to paving the way toward settling the territorial conflict. The impediments at play are: psychological resistance, historical experience and perception, entrenched ideologies, mutual delegitimization, and religious conviction. Together, these elements have locked both sides into immobile positions. The factors that maintain and enhance these impediments include: mutually heightened emotions such as fear, distrust, and enmity, an enduring sense of insecurity, and the continuing denial of the other's historical narrative. The operative result is stagnation of the peace process, violent outbursts, a deepening sense of insecurity, and political polarization on both sides.

Therefore, the development of a non-biased consensus-oriented dialogue at many levels is needed first to resolve the conflict. This would include officials and non-officials, civil society, educational institutions, the media, and peace advocacy organizations to engender public discussion to galvanize and understand each other's mindset, beliefs, and perceptions that have been formed over the years. This, needless to say, is a tall order because the current political environment in both camps is not conducive to a genuine dialogue and a process of reconciliation, which is a must and to which both sides must commit. But then, given the inevitability of coexistence under any and all circumstances, both sides are left with no choice but to come to terms with the reality that these impediments exist and must be addressed because they are at the core of the conflict and profoundly influence how Israelis and Palestinians perceive each other. The danger here is that the longer they wait, the more intractable their conflict becomes, with diminishing returns for both sides. Thus, to end the Israeli-Palestinian conflict at this juncture, we must consider the elements that inform the psychological impediments, their adverse impact on the peace process, and how to mitigate them to pave the way for a solution.

The Role of Psychological Resistance

On the surface, the deadlock in the Israeli-Palestinian peace process seems illogical and unsettling. After all, a *majority* of Israelis and Palestinians realize the inevitability of coexistence and *presumably* understand the general parameters of a negotiated peace agreement: a two-state solution based on the 1967 borders with some land swaps, Jerusalem would remain a united city (but a capital of two states), and the vast majority of Palestinian refugees would be compensated and/or resettled in the newly-created Palestinian state in the West Bank and Gaza Strip. These fundamental *imperatives*, coupled with all-encompassing security arrangements for Israel, represent what was on the negotiating table, in 2000 at Camp David and in 2008–2009 in Jerusalem and Ramallah, with each round coming closer to finalizing an agreement yet ultimately failing to do so. The question is why?

There are certain psychological concepts that are relevant to understanding the Israeli-Palestinian conflict; the concept of *illusion* is an essential one. In *The Future of an Illusion*, Freud offers the following definition: "We call a belief an illusion when a wish fulfillment is prominent in its motivation; in doing so we disregard its relation to reality, just as the illusion itself abjures confirmations."[v] An illusion, then, is not necessarily an error, unlike a delusion—that is, illusions "need not necessarily be false, i.e., unrealizable or in contradiction to reality."[vi] What is characteristic of illusions is that: 1) they are derived from deep human wishes, and 2) the belief is held (or would be held) in the absence of any compelling evidence, or good rational grounds, in its behalf.

It is impossible to deny that both Israelis and Palestinians are in the grip of very powerful illusions which only serve to prolong the conflict and prevent any mutual understanding. What are some of these illusions, or pipe-dreams, as the great American playwright Eugene O'Neill would call them? Following O'Neill, we can distinguish between the pipe-dreams of yesterday and the pipe-dreams of tomorrow. For example, the belief shared by many Israelis that they have a biblical right to the land (the ancient biblical lands of Judea and Samaria) and that God gave the Jews this land for all time is undoubtedly an illusion or a pipe-dream of yesterday. It is not affirmed because there is any real evidence for it, but because it satisfies a deep-seated psychological need for a God-given Jewish homeland. The belief that, by expanding the settlements Israel will augment its national security, is a pipe-dream of tomorrow. It is important to note how these illusions sustain and reinforce one another, and constitute a psychological barrier which is that much more impervious to critical reflection. Israel's illusions have served to create the *logic for occupation*, ultimately perpetuating the dehumanization of the Palestinians.

The Palestinians, for their part, are not without their own illusions. They believe, for example, that God has reserved the land for them, and appeal to the fact that they had inhabited the land for centuries. The presence of the al-Aqsa Mosque and the Dome of the

Rock in Jerusalem attest to their unmitigated historical and religious affinity to the Holy City. They also cling to the idea that they will someday return to the land of their forebears, as they have and continue to insist on the right of return of the Palestinian refugees, even though this has become a virtual impossibility. The Palestinians cling to their pipe-dreams of yesterday and tomorrow just as blindly and desperately as the Israelis, which leads to resistance to, and fear of, change.

These pipe dreams have contributed to making the Israeli-Palestinian conflict both chronic and intractable, as the various illusions are continuously and consciously nurtured by the daily encounters between the two sides. It would thus appear that the psychological concept of *resistance to change* is extremely relevant as well. First, a distinction is needed between resistance to persuasion, which is conscious and deliberate, and inner unconscious resistance to change. David Rabinowitz, one of Israel's leading psychiatrists, observes that the role of psychological resistance, an important function of unconscious resistance, is that it is protective in nature. In seeking bridging concepts that could link between the domains of psychology and politics in the Israeli-Palestinian conflict, it could be proposed that a collective mutual resistance to change protects a vulnerable identity. Compared to the stable and mature political identities of the American, British, and French nations, the political identities of both the Israeli and Palestinian peoples are, in a way, in their adolescence. Identities in this setting are more vulnerable, and the protagonists are naturally more defensive and resistant to change. By its very nature, the players must find it difficult (if not impossible) to articulate this publicly, as to do so is to admit to this vulnerability.

The idea of *psychological resistance to change* may well affect the political setting in general and the Israeli-Palestinian conflict in particular; it is closely connected to perceptions at many levels. Indeed, the psychological resistance provides protection for vulnerable identity formation in the Israeli-Palestinian conflict. It is this mindset, strengthened by historical experiences, which transcends the hundred-plus years since the Israeli-Palestinian conflict began. The individuals and groups, Israelis and Palestinians alike, have and continue to interpret the nature of their discord as "you versus me" in a prejudiced and selective way. In turn, this has stifled any new information and enabled the continuing resistance to change, which could shed new light on the nature and the substance of the conflict and help advance the peace process.

The idea of unconscious resistance to change in this setting links well to the view of perceptions driving the polarization in the conflict. Historical experience, which formulates perceptions, serves among other things to enhance the sense of identity of "who we really are," a formative collective assumption that sits at the bedrock of both key players and drives functional and dysfunctional behavior. As Rabinowitz puts it,

> the central benefit of this powerful unconscious resistance to change provides is the protection of a relatively vulnerable core identity [primary gains]… Secondary gains, however, are essentially the side-effects of the chronic polarization of this conflict: powerful allies offering material and political support [the U.S.' support of Israel and moderate Palestinians verses Iran's support for Palestinian militants such as Hamas], engaging in alluring narratives, public attention and useful alliances, etc.[vii]

In principle, such a mindset prevents either side from entertaining new ideas that might lead to compromises for a peaceful solution. The paradox here is that majorities on both sides *do* seek and want peace, knowing full well that this would require significant concessions, but are unable to reconcile the required concessions with embedded perceptions that have precluded these compromises as a result of resistance to change.

Therefore, to mitigate the Israeli-Palestinian conflict, we must first carefully look into the various elements that inform the psychological dimension of the conflict, and discuss how they impact the relationship between the two sides and what it would take to alleviate these psychological impediments as prerequisites to finding a solution.

Historical Experience and Perception

One of the critical parts that underlines the psychological aspect of the Israeli-Palestinian conflict are the scars that each side carries from their respective traumatic pasts. Their perceptions of each other were engendered by their independent historical experiences as they related to one another. Unfolding events—violence, mutual recrimination, etc.—between Israelis and Palestinians over the past seven decades, however, have made it virtually impossible for them to settle their differences. Maintaining an adversarial mindset toward each other has thus provided the justification and rationale to perpetuate their historical grievances through constant rancorous public narratives, placing the blame for the continuing discord on the other.

The Jews' experience throughout the diaspora was one filled with discrimination, persecution, antisemitism, and expulsion, culminating in the Holocaust. The genocide perpetrated during the Holocaust was surely something new in history—never before had a powerful state turned its immense resources to the industrialized manufacturing of corpses; never before had the extermination of an entire people been carried out with the swiftness of an assembly line. The fact that many Jews were prevented from avoiding death camps by being barred from immigrating to Palestine added yet another layer to the horrific experiences of the Jewish people. The Jews have carried the scars of this past with them and still hold to the view that it can happen again unless they remain vigilant and relentless in protecting themselves at any cost. With this past in mind, the establishment of the state of Israel was seen not only as the last refuge to provide protection for the Jewish people but also the realization and hope of both secular Zionism and biblical prophecy (i.e., the return of the Jews to their ancient homeland). Thus, religious and non-observant Jews believe this trust must be guarded with absolute and unwavering zeal.

Yet this historical sense of victimization and injustice has served to nurture the allegiance that each Israeli feels toward the state and each other with naturally engendered, negative emotional sentiments toward the enemy. From the Israeli perspective, the establishment of Israel on the heels of the Holocaust was seen (and continues to be viewed) as the last chance to create a refuge; they must therefore remain on guard to protect Jews' welfare and wellbeing wherever they may live and at whatever cost. This sense of being victimized resulted from an intentional infliction of harm in the past, universally viewed as utterly unjust and immoral—yet it has led to a lack of empathy toward perceived enemies. For example, it manifested itself in Israel shirking responsibility for the Palestinian refugee problem and violating human rights, all the while promoting self-righteousness.[viii] Hamas' unfathomable savagery resurrected memories of the Holocaust, and "never again" happened again. It evoked an unprecedented national fury that likewise led to the unparalleled onslaught on Gaza by the Israeli military forces that continues to inflict death and destruct unseen since the establishment of Israel in 1948.

Compounded, these conditions inherently endure, particularly when accompanied by extensive and continuing violence against Israel and growing concerns over national security. They are further strengthened by the Palestinians' public narrative, which openly promotes the rejection of the very existence of the state. The Palestinians, for their part, have hardly made any serious effort to comprehend and appreciate the psychological implications of the Jews' historical experience. Instead of understanding the Israeli mindset that was formed by the horrific past, the Palestinians have either denied the Holocaust altogether, or selfishly bemoaned that it did happen. It is not that the Palestinians should be held responsible for the Jews' historical tragedy, but still, they failed at a minimum to appreciate the Israelis' mindset in effectively dealing with the conflict.

For the Palestinians, the experience of the *Nakba* (the catastrophe), precipitated by the 1948 war, was no less calamitous. From their perspective, they were living in their own land, albeit for centuries under Ottoman rule and then under British Mandatory authority. They are absolutely convinced that during the 1948 war, they were forced out of their homes by Israelis, and although it is true that tens of thousands were forced out by the nascent Israeli forces, many were encouraged to leave by their Arab brethren and return "following the defeat of Israel" for the spoils.

Either way, over 750,000 Palestinians found themselves refugees after Israel's 1948 War of Independence, an experience that has lasted for decades and continues to endure, leaving an indelible impression on their psyche; currently, 5.9 million Palestinians are refugees.[ix] This traumatic experience served to bind Palestinians together in the same way that the Jews coalesced following the Holocaust, with each side believing their tragic historical experiences are unparalleled in scope and magnitude. The fact that the Arab states manipulated the Palestinian refugee problem over many decades to their advantage does not change the reality on the ground; it did not alter the Palestinians' mindset, their perception of what the Israelis have done, or their sentiment and disposition about their plight.

Frequent violent encounters between the two sides, especially after the 1967 war, further aggravated the Palestinian refugee problem. This war not only created another wave of refugees but also set the stage for a bloody confrontation during which many thousands lost their lives on both sides. The Israeli settlement project provided daily blows to Palestinian pride while demonstrating the futility of their efforts to stem Israeli encroachment on their territory, especially in the West Bank. The occupation and the repeated humiliation of the Palestinians further deepened their resolve to oppose the Israelis at whatever cost, but all was to no avail. The Israelis have proven to be a formidable foe, and the Palestinians' resentment, hatred, and animosity have naturally only increased.

Israelis have never fully understood the significance of what the Palestinians have been enduring, how this has impacted their psychological dispositions, and why they have shown no desire to reconcile their differences with Israel. Israelis often argue that since nearly 800,000 Jews left their homes (or as many believe, were forced out) across the Arab Middle East and North Africa and largely settled in Israel, the Palestinian refugees must be considered a *de facto swap with the Jewish refugees*.[x] This view not only dismisses the historical trauma experienced by the Palestinians, but also disregards their national aspirations to establish a homeland of their own, especially in light of the 1947 UN resolution (known as the Partition Plan) which called for separate Jewish and Palestinian states. This psychological fixation, reinforced by public narratives and education in schools,[xi] has prevented either side from coming to grips with the inevitability of coexistence under any circumstances.

Understanding the Israeli and Palestinian mindsets from the historical perspective is central to appreciating their respective resistances to change, which is detrimentally empowered by their historical experiences, especially if they continue to harbor political agendas that overshoot what they can realistically attain. That is, will their historical experiences, bequeathing a sense of mutual victimhood, be mitigated by the changing reality, or will they hold onto it until they achieve their objectives, however illusionary they may be? Indeed, do the Jewish peoples' and the Palestinians' unprecedented historical suffering—although they do not fall into the same category—somehow ontologically elevate them from "victims" to "Victims," guaranteeing them, and by extension contemporary Israelis and Palestinians, an unconditional status of moral untouchability?

The French philosopher Alain Badiou is right to suggest that we need to question the presumption that,

> like an inverted original sin, the grace of having been an incomparable victim can be passed down not only to descendants and to the descendants of descendants but to all who come under the predicate in question, be they heads of state or armies engaging in the severe oppression of those whose lands they have confiscated.[xii]

Indeed, the victim mentality has become a political tool for those who seek to promote their interests at the expense of the opposing political parties, not to mention the enemy.

The Palestinian culture of victimhood, on the other hand, was equally divisive in that it perpetuates the refugee problem by promoting a popular refusal of permanent resettlement. Palestinian leaders have also used it as a tool for public indoctrination,[xiii] ensuring that the Palestinian plight remains central to any political and social discourse. Palestinians and their leaders have carefully and systematically ingrained their victim mentality in the minds of one generation after another through the media, schools, and places of worship.

Israelis and Palestinians alike must become more self-critical in their use of victimhood; both sides need to realize that neither has a monopoly on the position of "the victim," and neither is granted a morally unimpeachable status as a consequence of their historical experiences or the shifting realities on the ground. The effect of adverse historical interaction, however, can be mitigated over time or reconciled through dialogue, eventually leading to changes in perception.

Notwithstanding their traumatic historical experiences, neither the Israelis nor the Palestinians can or should use history to foreshadow the present requirements to make peace. Historical experiences can be both instructive and destructive; a student of history must learn from past experiences but not emulate them and thus obscure a contemporary reality that can no longer be mitigated short of a catastrophe, in particular, Israeli-Palestinian coexistence. The Palestinians have every right to demand an end to the occupation and live with dignity; Israel has equal rights to satisfy its legitimate national security concerns. These two requirements are absolutely compatible and provide the only basis on which to build a structure of peaceful coexistence.

Without denying the Jews' and Palestinians' sense of victimhood, perpetuating their conflict ironically creates new generations of victims, robbing them of their future only because their elders want to cling to the historic past.

The Self-Imposed Ideological Siege

Juxtaposed to their historical experiences, the Israelis and Palestinians were moved by ideological bends informed by their national aspirations. Indeed, even a cursory review of the core ideologies of right-of-center Israelis and extremist Palestinians strongly suggests that, regardless of the dramatic changes in the political landscape since 1948, they remained ideologically besieged, making the conflict ever more intractable. Since Israelis and Palestinians know that coexistence under any scenario is inescapable, the question revolves around what it would take to modify their ideological bent to achieve a political solution to satisfy their mutual claims to the same land. The contradiction between Israel and the Palestinians in connection with "the land of Israel" as defined by right-of-center Israelis or "Palestine" as classified by Palestinian Islamists, is starkly evident in Likud's and Hamas' political platforms. The Likud Party Platform from the 15th Knesset (emphasis added) states,

> The Jewish communities in Judea, Samaria and Gaza are the realization of Zionist values… Settlement of the land is a clear expression of the unassailable right of the Jewish people to *the Land of*

Israel and constitutes an important asset in the defense of the vital interests of the State of Israel. The Likud will continue to strengthen and develop these communities and will prevent their uprooting.[xiv]

Hamas' 2006 electoral platform affirms that "Palestine is Arab and Muslim Land; Palestinians are one nation regardless of location; the Palestinian People are still in the process of National Liberation and have the right to use all means including armed struggle to achieve this goal."[xv]

Insisting on these principles amounts to a political dead end, as neither can force the other by any means to relinquish their claim to the same land short of catastrophe. The question is, can they modify their ideological stances without abandoning their core ideological positions? Ideology is often understood to be "the process whereby social life is converted to a natural reality" and, as such, ideology becomes "the indispensable medium in which individuals live out their relations to a social structure."[xvi] In either case, there are consistent efforts by Israeli zealots and Palestinian extremists to legitimize their respective ideologies by adopting a different strategy. As Terry Eagleton points out, "A dominant power may legitimate itself by *promoting* beliefs and values [ideology] congenial to it; *naturalizing* and *universalizing* such beliefs so as to render them self-evident and apparently inevitable; *denigrating* ideas which might challenge it; *excluding* rival forms of thought ... and *obscuring* social reality in ways convenient to itself."[xvii]

Thus, to understand the depth of the Israeli and Palestinian contradictory positions, we must look briefly at the evolutionary development of the conflict from its inception. The Jewish community sought to establish a state of its own early in the twentieth century, which was subsequently granted by the UN partition plan in 1947 (UN General Assembly Resolution 181), thereby legitimizing the Zionist ideology to establish a Jewish Home in the ancient biblical land. The Palestinians refused the partition plan along with the rest of the Arab states, who waged a war on the nascent state resulting in the loss of more territory and the mass exodus of Palestinian refugees. Although the Palestine Liberation Organization (PLO), which led the Palestinian revolutionary movement, and Israel recognized each other at the Oslo Accords in 1993, Hamas (which was established in 1987) continues to object to Israel's existence altogether.

Immediately following the 1967 war, Israel offered to return all the captured territories (except East Jerusalem); the offer was rebuffed by the Arab League. Convening in Khartoum, Sudan, in the same year, the Arab League submitted their three infamous NOs: no peace, no recognition, and no negotiations with Israel.[xviii] That response was seen by the Israelis as an outright rejection by the Arab states of Israel's very existence, despite the Israelis' willingness to relinquish the captured territories, which continues to resonate in the minds of many Israelis. In the process, both sides moved to act to enforce their ideological beliefs. The Israelis consistently pursued settlement policies, and the Palestinians, especially Hamas, held onto their militant resistance. The continuing violent confrontations, in particular the Second Intifada (2000–2005) and the Israeli crackdown on Palestinian terror attacks (in 2014, 2018, and 2021 in particular), further deepened the gulf between them while intensifying mutual distrust.

Ideological and political factionalism in both camps has made the conflict increasingly intractable. Since the creation of Israel, political parties have mushroomed, reaching at one time more than 25 parties. As a result, all governments have been coalition-based, consisting of several deeply conflicted parties with little consensus on how to address the Palestinian problem and the disposition of the occupied territories. In every election between twelve and fifteen parties pass the qualifying threshold of 3.25 percent of the electoral vote and are guaranteed at least four out 120 members of the Knesset.[3] The right-of-center parties still represent nearly half of the Israeli electorate and hold significant sway over settlement policy. What started with the building of a few settlements to protect Jerusalem has now become a major enterprise embedded in the ideology that "the land of Israel" is the Jews' inherent historical land. The settlers' movement became a powerhouse and now enjoys tremendous influence on any government, regardless of its political position and ideological leaning.

Factionalism within the Palestinians has made it also impossible to speak in one voice. Following the 1993 Oslo Accords, however, a growing majority of Palestinians began to realize that they must find a way to co-exist with Israel, particularly in light of the PLO's agreement in Oslo to "recognize their mutual legitimate and political rights, and strive to live in peaceful coexistence and mutual dignity and security."[xix] Hamas, which assumed control of Gaza in 2007, continues to struggle to find a way to reconcile with the reality of Israel. Yet despite this growing pragmatic view, a significant constituency of Israelis and Palestinians continues to reject one another on ideological grounds.

The question is how to reconcile ideological ethos with certain irreversible realities on the ground—Israeli-Palestinian coexistence—and their mutual claim to the same territory. History and experiences suggest that, regardless of how deep an ideological conviction may be, it cannot be sustained if it does not enshrine justice, fairness, and human rights at its very core. An ideological shift will become inevitable due to the seven factors below.

Inevitable Failure

Notwithstanding the success of right-of-center parties in Israel and Hamas' continued resistance, both will realize that *failure is imminent*. The falsity of the Israeli position to help to legitimate a dominant political order and the socially useful (or necessary) illusion has and will continue to backfire. Indeed, there are certain condi-

---

3   See https://m.knesset.gov.il/en/about/pages/knessetwork.aspx.

tions on the ground which neither side can change, in particular *their coexistence*. Ideological divergence notwithstanding, their fate is intertwined, and they must choose between reconciliation or mutual self-destruction.

Changing Political Wind

The changing political landscape among Israelis and Palestinians suggests that both camps are undergoing a gradual ideological shift. Fatah came to the conclusion that violence as a means by which to achieve political objectives has failed and began to focus on a solution by peaceful means. Hamas, however, has adopted a two-track approach. On the one hand, they began to signal their readiness to establish a Palestinian state based on the 1967 borders under condition of no war and no peace (*hudna*), while maintaining a military approach (armed struggle) as an option, primarily for domestic consumption, on the other.[xx]

Arresting Shift to the Right

The political landscape in Israel indicates that there has been a further shift to the right and right-of-center. While hardcore ideological positions continue and systematic distortions of communication (for example, in connection with national security and its linkage to the final borders) do exist, the new political map may well slow the settlements' incursion due to the growing strength of the constituency that supports the status quo.

The Demographic Factor

As a result of the rapidly changing demographic ratios between Israelis and Palestinians, Israel is facing an imminent danger of losing its Jewish majority.[xxi] Sooner than later, Israel must choose between a true democracy with a sustainable Jewish majority or a democracy in name only, as discrimination against the Palestinians by the Israelis becomes a tool of necessity to maintain its Jewish dominance. Israel refuses to relinquish much of the West Bank, which will unavoidably lead to an apartheid state that *de facto* already exists, inviting international censure, condemnation, and sanctions.

The Failure of Armed Struggle

Unless a negotiated agreement with Israel is reached, no armed struggle will dislodge Israel from its current position. The peace process, however, has evolved to a point where the PA has given up on armed struggle and instead resorted to unilateral actions, guided by the belief that it is the only way to advance its goal and force Israel's hand. The Palestinians were successful in their efforts to upgrade their diplomatic status to "non-voting observer state" at the UN General Assembly, and Hamas, though it occasionally challenges Israel by the use of force, also recognizes that armed struggle to destroy Israel has now become beyond their reach.[4] Despite Hamas' devastating attack on October 7th, Israel's massive retaliation has only further demonstrated the futility of their armed struggle against Israel.

No Gains, Only Increased Vulnerability

In the clash of ideologies, however, there comes a point where neither side is making any gains but is actually becoming increasingly vulnerable. Israel is increasingly under scrutiny and the Palestinians are watching the territory of their future state usurped to make room for more settlements. The forecast for both sides appears to be bleak and further worsening. In the long term, however, Israel will end up on the losing side as the Palestinian cause will continue to garner international support.

The Potential for Massive Violent Explosion

Given the simmering situation and the frustration over the stalemate, repeated violent eruptions are inevitable. Ideology aside, the average Palestinian is edging ever closer to challenging the occu-

---

4   This is based on a number of personal conversations I had with Hamas officials over a number of years.

pation. They understand that Israel has the capacity to quell such a violent challenge, but still, they are prepared to emulate their counterparts in Syria and other Arab countries, who have sacrificed themselves for their freedom. For Israel, this would represent a major dilemma as cracking down on Palestinian demonstrators will evoke international outrage, as the majority of the world views the Palestinians as the victims of immoral occupation.

Israelis and Palestinians can certainly introduce a modified version of their ideological bent, as the reality allows for a gradual shift without sacrificing their ideological principles and without losing face. The Palestinians can establish a state on a part of their homeland and come to terms with Israel's existence within its current borders. The Israelis must accept the fact that Israel will have to negotiate from the basis of the 1967 borders with some land swaps of approximately five to seven percent to accommodate for the three blocs of settlements (commonly acknowledged as Ma'ale Adumim, Gush Etzion, and Betar Illit, although the exact configuration is open for negotiation). This is not to suggest that all issues will readily be resolved, but the realization that coexistence is not negotiable will eventually trump the ideological ethos of both sides. The alternative is the continuation of this self-imposed ideological siege, which is bound to fail the test of time at a price that neither side can afford to pay.

The Peril of Mutual Delegitimization

In Israel, a powerful right-of-center constituency rejects the notion that Palestinians constitute a nation with the right to establish an independent state of their own. Among Palestinians, powerful groups like Hamas and Islamic Jihad likewise reject the premise that Jews comprise a nation with the right to an independent state; even those Palestinians who concede this issue certainly do not feel that the Jewish state should be erected on Palestinian land. To further propagate their respective positions, both Israeli and Palestinian rejectionists *are engaged in mutual and systematic dele-*

gitimization of the other. Although the 1993–1994 Oslo Accords presumably changed (at least to a certain degree) the nature of the relationship between the two sides through mutual recognition, they did not fundamentally mitigate the doubt each side held or altered their predisposed perception of the other. That is, the mutually embedded rejectionist sentiment in their respective psyches creates insurmountable resistance to change, especially by inciting deliberate actions that further reinforce the rejection of the other.

In probing the psychological barriers to change, we must also pay close attention to the manner in which *helplessness and radical vulnerability* inhibit the positive transformation of the *status quo*. Helplessness arises when one's relation to the self or to the world is systematically undone at the hands of another, "but undone so thoroughly and unconditionally that the victim loses any sense of being able to determine himself, his immediate environment, or, thus, his relations to the world in general: you experience yourself as in a state of existential helplessness."[xxii] While the sense of being exposed and constitutively vulnerable is doubtless more severe among Palestinians, we should not hastily assume that because Israel is an immensely powerful state, its citizens do not also share in this experience: constant concerns over personal security and chronic fear of change are more than enough to foster vulnerability of the self among Israelis.

The leadership on both sides have too often sought to instill public resentment by maligning public narratives, and denying the rights and humanity of the other. Palestinians, for example, blame Israel for the suffering caused by the refugee problem, while Israel blames the Palestinians for the never-ending terrorism and violence, especially the Second Intifada that stunned Israelis and shattered any remaining residue of trust. Of course, the October 7th attack only reinforced the Israelis' distrust of the Palestinians.

Refutations of the other's public narratives, however, are not limited to statements or announcements made by officials. For example, Israelis view the Palestinian insistence on the refugees' right of return as an effort to obliterate the Jewish identity of the state. Similarly, Palestinians consider Israel's settlement building throughout the West Bank a gross encroachment on their land for the express purpose of denying them the opportunity to establish their own state. By insisting publicly only on their respective rights, both sides view the other's actions merely as efforts to delegitimize and undermine the other.

The campaign of mutual delegitimization, not limited to the political and public domain, has developed into a culture that permeates all social strata, particularly education and the media. This aspect of delegitimization is more troubling than any other in that it not only denies each other's rights in the eyes of the contemporary general public but also poisons the next generation of adults, who are indoctrinated from childhood to reject the other. Palestinian textbooks have distorted and continue to distort the factual historical account of what actually happened between Israelis and Palestinians and how the current situation came to pass.[xxiii] Palestinian geography books fail to delineate Israel on maps, and teachers that express hostility seed in the minds of young students deep-rooted hatred for Jews, perpetuating the delegitimization of Israel and making it extremely difficult to mitigate the damage when Palestinian children come of age.

In Israel, new history textbooks were, in fact, published and introduced into Israeli junior and senior high schools in 1999 after the Oslo peace agreement was signed. While these new textbooks attempted to offer a more balanced account of the Israeli-Arab conflict than previous publications, they still presented a typical nationalistic narrative, which left little room for recognizing the legitimacy of the Palestinians.[xxiv] Thus, instead of using the classroom to promote each other's rights and plights, schools on both sides of the border have become laboratories for manufacturing perceptions useful in the delegitimization of the other. Of course, these perceptions are further and frequently reinforced by violent events, perpetuating cultures of hatred at home, at the temple, and in the mosque.

ALON BEN-MEIR

In Israel, where a largely free press is a given and both print and
electronic media run the gamut from extreme-right to extreme-left,
many news outlets openly criticize the government for its treatment of and policy toward the Palestinians. The same cannot at
all be said about Palestinian media. This is particularly problem-
atic because the criticism and condemnation of Israel, regardless
of how justified it may be, becomes institutionalized, leading to
the formation of a popular mindset that makes reconciliation with
Israel all the more difficult. To be sure, conscious efforts toward
delegitimizing the other not only cause suffering and harm to both
sides but also permits and justifies continuing moral infractions
against the opposing faction. Delegitimization sustains conflict,
minimizes concessions made by both sides, and inadvertently
leads to heightened resistance to change and renewed violence.

In weighing the psychological impediments to change, the significance of the process of *socialization* cannot be ignored, especially
if we want to understand how both sides are able to justify moral
infractions against the other. That is, we need to explore not only
the forces that push people into performing violent and oppressive
acts but also the psychological forces that contribute to the weakening of moral restraints that routinely check individuals against
performing acts they would normally find reprehensible. The 2012
documentary *The Gatekeepers*,[5] about the Shin Bet (Israel's General Internal Security Service), is to be commended for raising pre-
cisely this issue, among others.

At least three processes involved in socialization deserve to be
mentioned. The first process is *authorization*. Rather than recognizing oneself as an independent moral agent, the individual feels
that they are participating in a "transcendent mission," one that
relinquishes them of the responsibility to make their own moral
choices. The second is *routinization*, the process through which
an action is organized and divided among numerous individuals
such that "there is no opportunity for raising moral questions and

5   See https://www.youtube.com/watch?v=J1N93pFcopE.

28

making moral decisions … Each individual carries out routine tasks without having to think of the overall product created by these tasks."[xxv] What should be emphasized here is that the aura of professionalism permits the insider to perceive the process not as the brutal treatment of other human beings "but as the routine application of specialized knowledge and skills."[xxvi] Finally, *dehumanization*, whereby the other is systematically excluded from the moral community to which one belongs; it becomes unnecessary for agents to regard their relationship to the other as ethically significant. In short, the victim of dehumanization is denied any moral consideration.

Although a relative majority of Israelis seek a resolution to the conflict based on a two-state solution supported by many think tanks and a wide range of media outlets, a demeaning attitude toward the Palestinians signifying they do not deserve or cannot be treated as equals pervades the culture. In this way, Israelis have become complacent toward the occupation, and content to ignore the urgency to create a Palestinian state. Israeli indifference toward the Palestinians' plight has become second nature, creating a mindset among Israelis that blames the Palestinians for their problems.

I believe that the category of "soul death" (originally proposed as a way of thinking about the social-psychological impact of slavery) is entirely relevant to understanding the suffering of the Palestinians. Applying this concept means coming to grips with the real and awful impact of being utterly overpowered by another, of having one's home ransacked and one's village arbitrarily divided by the building of fences (presumably to prevent terrorism), of having one's house raided in the middle of the night, terrifying women and children, and of losing the sense of having any control over one's life. Not unlike African Americans under Jim Crow or South Africans under apartheid, the Palestinians have seen their humanity systematically denied by the forces of occupation. Yet Israel continues to ignore the grievances and suffering of those whose lands it confiscated, the consequence of this state-sanctioned delegitimization being little short of soul death for Palestinians.

The ever-present possibility of terrible and unpredictable violence not only destroys the hope that the situation will someday be resolved, but also increases the sense of shame, despondency, and the will to retaliate to make the other suffer. The trauma suffered by the victim of deliberate violence lingers on in its aftermath as a part of the victim's very sense of self, and "it is that which makes such helplessness existential and categorical."[xxvii] The point here is that this sense of existential helplessness has and will continue to grow among the Palestinians (*and* Israelis) if the conflict is allowed to continue indefinitely.

Whether we are talking about the settler who will stop at nothing to maintain control of the land or the militant Palestinian who is sworn to the destruction of Israel, both see themselves as pursuing a divinely authorized mission, the fulfillment of which absolves them of any moral culpability. Categories of zealotry consistently and accurately apply to both Israelis and Palestinians, while blind refusal of reality by influential voices on both sides obscures the voices of those on the fringes seeking to reach a solution. This will only result in further alienation and perilous delegitimization of the other and is certainly the recipe for "Mutually Assured Destruction."

Religious Conviction and Reality

Finally, what has dramatically aggravated the Israeli-Palestinian psychological impediment is the religious component which has created a certain mindset that further complicates the struggle and adds to its intransigence. Both Jews and Muslims alike have mystified the struggle, projecting cosmic significance and introducing national and religious pride into the equation. In addition is the fact that from a religious perspective there exist structures—the Temple Mount (*Haram al-Sharif*) where the al-Aqsa Mosque and the Dome of the Rock are situated, juxtaposed to the Wailing Wall—which are equally holy to both sides. But since there is hardly any Israeli or Palestinian who can conceivably contemplate the destruction of these holy sites to benefit the other, short of ensuing a catastrophic religious war, settling their religious dispute based on the reality on the ground *becomes the only viable option.* For this reason, Israel and the Palestinians have little choice but to reconcile their religious narratives and make Jerusalem the microcosm of peaceful coexistence rather than a source of perpetual conflict and violence.

The Israelis' own religious narrative is one that is based on the biblical connection of the Jewish people to the land of their forefathers. As Prime Minister Netanyahu reminded the U.S. Congress in his May 24, 2011 address, "This is the land of our forefathers, the Land of Israel, to which Abraham brought the idea of one God, where David set out to confront Goliath, and where Isaiah saw a vision of eternal peace."[xxviii]

Most Israelis believe that no distortion of history can deny the religious component that has created a bond, spanning thousands of years, between the Jewish people and the biblical Jewish land. Since the ancient Hebrews are not historically the same thing as Jews—not culturally and not even religiously—the Hebraic tradition of 3,000 years ago, having little similarity to modern Jewry, hardly means an inheritance in land for Jews. That said, and with religious faith requiring no evidence, for many Israelis it is simply unacceptable to completely relinquish control of the West Bank, known in ancient times as the biblical lands of Judea and Samaria. From that perspective, it is inconceivable in particular for them to surrender their holiest shrine, especially the Wailing Wall (the outer wall of the Second Temple), allowing Jerusalem to be governed or fall under the jurisdiction of any other peoples or an international governing body. As a result, despite all Israelis happily accepting the 1947 UN partition plan, they have always held onto the dream of eventually repossessing all of Jerusalem, east and west.

This unique attachment and affinity to the holy city, which has for millennia symbolized the Jewish sense of redemption, created a powerful motivation to capture the city when it came within their grasp during the Six Day War in 1967. The fall of Jerusalem in the wake of the war remains an unmatched event and came to symbolize absolute Jewish redemption. This historic development created a renewed awakening that vindicated the religious premise that was embedded in the Jewish psyche for centuries. The realization of what was believed to be a far-fetched dream under the most difficult of circumstances was now seen as the work of the Almighty that no force can alter. Considered in this light, we can understand or at least provide a framework for the zeal of those who are committed to keeping all of Jerusalem and much, if not all, of the West Bank under Israeli jurisdiction— they see that as the fulfillment not only of God's promise but God's very will.

What further explains the mindset of these believers is that no man can reason to the contrary of God's plan. Regardless of the facts on the ground (the existence of the Palestinians and their claim to East Jerusalem), the Jews in and outside Israel consider it their obligation to do everything in their power to fulfill God's will, which transcends humanity's narrow perception of reality. This explains the position of many Israeli Jews who see no wrongdoing in building new and expanding existing settlements in the West Bank, particularly in East Jerusalem.

From the settlers' perspective, the majority of whom believe they are merely fulfilling what God has ordained; for the Jews to earn the right to hold onto Jerusalem they must prove that they are worthy to repossess it, even if this includes the suppression of the Palestinians and defiance of the international community. For these reasons, regardless of how powerful the resistance of Palestinians, other Arab and Muslim states, and much of the international community to the Israeli position, the religious mandate trumps any and all opposition: the settlers view themselves as pursuing God's mission and must demonstrate unshakable resolve, tenacity, and willingness to make any sacrifice necessary before He once again grants them the Promised Land.

With the recapture of Jerusalem and control asserted over the West Bank, what seemed to be destined to remain only a pipe-dream was suddenly transformed into a reality. This development was strengthened by concerted efforts toward creating permanent anchors on the ground through building settlements and infrastructure needed to augment continuity. These efforts led to the gradual galvanization of intergroup factions, especially the settlement movement, which has gained tremendous political sway and uses it effectively to block any policy or action on the ground that could compromise the settlement enterprise. Indeed, successive Israeli governments, regardless of their ideological leaning, have bent to the settlers' whims.

The expansion of the settlements, along with the prospect of building the young Jewish state on the entire mythological ancient homeland, has created this particular and most powerful psychological disposition. As this religious mindset has become even further embedded in the Israeli psyche, the nearly decisive power of the settlement movement has made it increasingly difficult to contemplate a return to the 1967 borders, with or without some land swaps.

Due to religious convictions tied to Islam's third holiest shrines in Jerusalem—the al-Aqsa Mosque and the Dome of the Rock, or *Haram al-Sharif*—Muslim leaders, like their Jewish counterparts, will not compromise on Jerusalem or on recovering much of the West Bank's land. Many Muslim scholars believe that Muhammad made his Journey from Mecca to *Masjid Al-Aqsa* (literally, "furthest mosque") in Jerusalem before he ascended to heaven. Although the al-Aqsa Mosque was built long after the prophet's death, Surah 17:1 states that Mohammad visited the site where the al-Aqsa Mosque was subsequently erected. This belief is certainly not limited to the Palestinians but shared by all Muslims, further complicating any solution to the future of Jerusalem. Like the Israelis, the Palestinians too have shown absolutely no flexibility in this regard.

One other difficulty that adds to the psychological impediment in relation to Jerusalem is the Palestinians' sense of ownership, which has been uninterrupted for centuries. Although Arabs have lived with Jews in relative peace throughout the centuries and under various Muslim governances until the vast majority of Jews living in Arab countries left or were expelled by the 1950s, Jews were treated as second-class citizens, who in turn largely accepted subordination in order to maintain peaceful relations. Centuries of Arab perception of Jews as a subordinated minority make it nearly impossible for them to accept Jews as equals, not to mention as a superior power forcefully usurping land they consider their own. The Palestinians' position in connection with Jerusalem and the entire West Bank must therefore be seen in this context as well.

Further consideration of the Arab view of Islam as the final revelation of the three major Abrahamic religions (including Judaism and Christianity) and of Muhammad as the last prophet accentuate Palestinian and Muslim unwillingness to compromise in what they believe to be their inherent religious duty to obey God's final revelation. Here again, the psychological barrier embedded in religious precepts creates a mindset willing to defy reality. Yet no one is permitted to challenge God's decree and Muhammad's edict.

Freud made the claim that religious beliefs should be viewed as wish-fulfillments—or beliefs chiefly motivated by deep-seated human wishes, i.e., illusions. When we look without bias at the beliefs held by so many on both sides of the Israeli-Palestinian conflagration, who could not help but agree with his assessment? Of course, an illusion could turn out to be true: the belief that the Jewish people would someday establish a mighty state on the very same land where their ancient ancestors once lived was certainly illusory only a hundred years ago. Even if we agree with Freud that religious beliefs are illusions, we cannot agree with his prediction that such illusions are likely to wither away any time soon.

In the final analysis, religion has been and will most likely continue to be the repository of our most deeply held wishes and beliefs, as it is for many Israelis and Palestinians alike. For believers on both sides, religion constitutes nothing less than the very substance of their lives, the core of their existence and world-view. The question is: can both parties be brought to reconcile their beliefs to the changed reality on the ground? Neither Israelis nor Palestinians can be expected to undermine their most cherished religious convictions, but if disappointments are unavoidable, the convictions recognized and honored by the other side and by the global community must be adapted and reinterpreted in light of new and undeniable conditions. To take a crucial example, while neither side can forsake Jerusalem without compromising their religion, they can begin to accommodate their aspirations to the prospect of Jerusalem as the dual capital of two sovereign and independent states. Perhaps then the historical and religious commitments of both sides can be respected. It is only through mutual realization of spiritual hopes and ideals that Israelis and Palestinians will reconcile and see the fulfillment of God's promise of peace—and that is surely no mere pipe-dream.

In closing, as we have seen, the prerequisite to settling the Israeli-Palestinian conflict is the need to mitigate these impediments to pave the way for a peaceful solution to their conflict. This certainly is, as stated earlier, a very tall order because nearly eight decades of violent conflict have taken their toll, leaving both sides psychologically wounded, suspicious of one another, impervious to the other's pain, and decreasingly inclined to make the necessary concessions to reach a peace agreement. The general consensus among many Israelis, Palestinians, and foreign observers has always been that the *status quo* is not sustainable, which tragically was demonstrated once again with Hamas' savagery on the seventh of October.

THE MUTUAL CURSE OF THE OCCUPATION

To understand the disastrous impact of the occupation on Israelis and Palestinians alike, one has to consider a crucial statistic: nearly 80 percent of Israelis today and over 90 percent of all Palestinians were born after Israel's 1967 capture of the West Bank and Gaza.[6] Just think of *the psychological, emotional, and everyday implications of this shattering reality* and the way it has shaped the two communities, how they have been affected by it, and how they view each other.

In September 2022, I spoke with the father of a soldier who at the time was serving in the West Bank to find out what the situation on the ground was like at that time. The following story was related to me regarding a conversation the soldier had with a Palestinian boy, which demonstrates the situation under which millions have grown up in the occupied territories.

> The soldier ventured to ask a 13-year-old Palestinian boy how he feels about his life, about the Israeli Jews, and about the occupation in general. The young boy hesitated at first to answer, fearing that if he said something derogatory to an Israeli soldier real harm will come his way. Sensing the boy's hesitancy, the soldier gave assurances that he would not be harmed. "Do you really want to know?" the boy asked. Without waiting for an answer, the boy continued, "My grandfather passed away at the age of 64, humiliated and jobless. He felt ashamed because he could not provide for his family and the last few words he said to my father from his death bed were, *'don't let them do to you what they have done to me.'* My father knew only too well what his father went through under occupation, as he lived

---

6   Figures are approximate and compiled from demographic data published by *The World Factbook.*

it from the time he was nine years old.

"My father's lot has not been much better. Our little house was raided by Israeli security forces three times; every time I woke up terrified, screaming, hoping that it was just an awful nightmare. Then I realized it was all too real. I can still see my mother cowering in fear, warned by the soldiers not to scream as they handcuffed my father and shoved him out the door. Each time he spent several days in prison and was subsequently released without being charged with any crime." With tears rolling down his cheeks, the boy looked straight at the soldier's eyes and said: "You have crushed his dignity; he lives in fear not knowing when he will be incarcerated again. Soldiers like you have instilled dread in his heart, making his life miserable, and yes, after our olive trees, which are our main source of livelihood, were uprooted by soldiers just like you, my father now is a broken man, struggling day in and day out to make ends meet.

"Do you want to know more? I will tell you. Now you are robbing me of *my future*, you treat me and my friends like stray dogs. Why? *What have I done?* Even if my grandfather or my father committed a crime, *why should I suffer* for their transgression? I can never forgive or forget, how can I? I am the product of a third generation of despairing Palestinians suffering under the harsh reality of the occupation. I do not know where I will be in five or ten years, maybe in prison or dead, like the 300 Palestinians who were shot to death by Israeli forces last year alone, but I know one thing, I want revenge for the all the injustices and the daily humiliation that we endure."

While this is a relation of the conversation and not an exact transcription of what occurred, based on what I know firsthand, it still accurately conveys the reality in the West Bank and reflects the thoughts and feelings of this young boy, whose fear and anger are real. This heart-wrenching story is but one of thousands of similar tales you hear throughout the West Bank. The Palestinians are enduring the pain, agony, and humiliation of the occupation every day and everywhere they go with no relief in sight. Each day at the crack of dawn, Palestinians encounter new dismaying incidents that have become the norm: forced evictions of Palestinians from homes where their families lived for generations, confiscation of land allegedly needed for security, the incarceration of innocent youths without charges, or daily harassment and violence by settlers against ordinary Palestinians, and suspected militants brutally treated without any proof of wrongdoing. Palestinians are presumed guilty and the burden is on them to prove their innocence. Indeed, no Palestinian can escape the stench of occupation wherever they may go or hide.

Israel, of course, does not want any of its chilling human rights violations to be reported or exposed. Human Rights Watch reports that Israel is "carrying out an unprecedented all-out assault on human rights advocates … on August 18 [2022], Israeli authorities raided the offices of seven prominent Palestinian civil society organizations."[xxix] And in a separate incident, Israeli security forces detained Nasser Nawaj'ah, a field researcher for the Israeli rights group B'Tselem, who stated after his arrest,

> It is not surprising that Israel goes after people who document the injustices it commits in the Occupied Territories and work to expose it. The violence of the Israeli forces is nothing new—it is a daily part of my work and of life for all Palestinians in the Occupied Territories ... The fate of human rights advocacy in Israel and Palestine may well hang in the balance.[xxx]

It is not hard to imagine the impact of Israel's treatment of the Palestinians in the occupied territories. The Palestinians have become embittered, resentful, and intensely hateful. What Israel is doing is deliberately provoking the Palestinians through its harsh treatment and thus, directly or inadvertently, nurturing Palestinian militancy, which encourages violent resistance that Israel can readily contain. Then Israel turns around and accuses Palestinian youths of being militant and bent on killing Israelis, using these largely false allegations to tighten its control over the territories in the name of national security and to justify the continuing occupation. As such, successive Israeli governments, especially those led by right-wing leaders, such as Prime Minister Netanyahu, who is remembered for repeatedly insisting that "there will be no Palestinian state under my watch,"[7] contend that, given the Palestinians' militancy and deep enmity toward Israel, no Israeli government can allow for the creation of a Palestinian state which will pose an existential threat to the country.

The Curse of Normalizing the Occupation

This is the reality and the tragic consequences of the occupation for the Palestinians, but it is equally tragic for the Israelis, albeit in a different way and with different implications for Israelis as individuals and for Israel itself as a Jewish state. The normalization of the occupation is a curse many Israelis still are oblivious to, even though it is dangerously eroding the moral foundation on which Israel was established. The vast majority of Israelis who grew up with the occupation generally pay no heed to what is happening in the occupied territories. Even though centrist and left-of-center media outlets and scores of human rights organizations are sounding the alarm, they have done little to make Israelis in general more conscientious and concerned—not only in terms of what is happening in the territories, but also as to how the occupation is affecting their own character.

---

7   See Eliott C. McLaughlin, "Israel's PM Netanyahu: No Palestinian state on my watch," CNN, March 16, 2015, https://www.cnn.com/2015/03/16/middleeast/israel-netanyahu-palestinian-state/index.html.

Following over a millennium of segregation, persecution, expulsion, and death, Israel was created to provide a home, a refuge for the Jews to live in safety with their fellow Jews without fear of what tomorrow may hold. Israel's creation was made necessary precisely because of the untold suffering to which the Jews have been subjected for centuries throughout the diaspora. One would think that the last thing that Israel as a Jewish state would do is subject other people to the same dehumanizing treatment *and thereby forfeit the moral imperative that gave rise to its very being.*

For tens of thousands of Israeli boys and girls, like their fathers and even grandfathers, the West Bank is an extension of Israel proper. They have been taught and indoctrinated with the belief that this land was bequeathed to them exclusively by the Almighty for eternity and that the Jews have come back to reclaim what is inherently theirs. The Palestinians are portrayed as the perpetual enemy not to be trusted or reconciled with. This dehumanization of the Palestinians escapes much of the Israeli public's consciousness. They are temporarily awakened when a violent incident by a Palestinian against Israeli Jews or another mini-war with Hamas occurs, but it is soon forgotten once Israel's security forces ruthlessly deal with the situation so as to teach a would-be Palestinian extremist individual or group a lesson they won't forget. The frequent violent flareup between Israel and Hamas and Islamic Jihad in Gaza offers just another example that demonstrates this unfortunate state of affairs.

Despite the Jews' long and troubling history, even after attaining their own independence at an unimaginable cost, a growing majority of Israeli Jews fail to understand that *they are not really free as long as they dismiss the Palestinians' right to self-determination.* The normalization of occupation has made the Israelis increasingly numb to the Palestinians' plight, and they have forgotten how it feels to live in servitude with little or no hope for a better and more promising tomorrow. However, when this indifference to the pain of others becomes a way of life, it robs the individual Israeli of his or her own humanity and dignity, which are central to a wholesome existence. To be sure, the abuse of Palestinians in the occupied territories has become generational, and with every new generation that passes, the Israelis are becoming more accustomed to a reality that further debases their own humanity.

Moreover, although a growing majority of Israelis can now live with the occupation without much concern about how it might evolve, some want to end it, knowing how destructive it is to both Israelis and Palestinians alike. Yet many remain apprehensive about discussing it publicly, fearing accusations of being anti-Israel and pro-Palestinian. To be sure, the occupation has created a social schism between the two sides. There are those right-wing Israelis who have sworn to hold onto the territories at any cost and prevent the Palestinians from ever establishing an independent state of their own. And there are those who are against the occupation not only because they are motivated by humanitarian concerns but also because they want to protect Israel's democracy, which is rapidly deteriorating, and because they consider the occupation to be a threat to their national security.

Indeed, Israel applies two sets of laws in the occupied territories: one for Israeli Jews who enjoy the rights, benefits, and protection of Israeli citizenship, and another set of discriminatory military laws that apply to the Palestinians and entail a completely different rule of jurisprudence which is the antithesis to democracy. As such, *Israel has become a* de facto *apartheid state*, intensely disappointing and perturbing to its friends and deeply loathed and resisted by its enemies.

Thus, when the historically persecuted Jews become the persecutors, Israel not only undermines its moral legitimacy but exposes itself to critics who wrongly seek to minimize or even deny the Holocaust, the horror of which motivated the moral claim to the establishment of a Jewish state on a part of its ancestral homeland.

In August 2022, when PA President Abbas met with German Chancellor Olaf Scholz, he said that Israel committed "50 massacres; 50

Holocausts" against the Palestinians.[xxxi] Even though Israel's egregious human rights violations against the Palestinians are totally unacceptable, comparing them to the Holocaust in multiples of 50 is beyond reprehensible and must be condemned in the strongest terms. However, it shows how cavalierly the greatest tragedy inflicted on any people is being referenced by President Abbas, no less, who presumably seeks peace with Israel. Furthermore, anyone who cares about Israel but denies that the rise of antisemitism is not attributable at least in part to the occupation and the way the Palestinians are treated is delusional. They render Israel and the Jews, wherever they reside, a terrible disservice as they obscure the disastrous ramifications of the occupation.

Although this internal discord among Israeli Jews in connection with the occupation has not come, as of yet, to a boil, it remains potent and is bound to surface in one form or another, especially given Israel's endemic political polarization. Every Israeli wants to be the prime minister, but no official or laymen has any plan or vision whatsoever as to how to engender the national consensus that will bring an end to the occupation and address the Palestinians' legitimate claim for an independent state, *provided that it coexists in peace and security side-by-side with Israel.*

The above review of the occupation and its severe adverse impact on both Palestinians and Israelis leaves little room for speculation as to whether or not the time is ripe for a solution to their conflict. The Israeli occupation is a ticking time bomb that could explode with no warning: any violent incident could ignite a conflagration because the legitimate anger and sense of injustice among the Palestinians is simmering just under the surface and is bound to eventually explode. Meanwhile, the Israelis' complacency and self-assurance that they can indefinitely maintain and live with the *status quo* is obscuring the looming disaster. The shock of October 7th bitterly awakened a growing number of Israelis to the reality that occupation is a cancer that will consume the Israelis from within to a point of no return unless they unless they end it.

The continuing occupation made it impossible to resolve the four most intractable conflicting issues between Israel and the Palestinians: namely, the Palestinian refugees, the Israeli settlements, Jerusalem, and national security. The failure to address these issues over the past several decades further intensified the Israeli-Palestinian conflict, precipitating frequent outbursts of violence and mini wars, which tragically culminated with Hamas' October 7th attack.

The Palestinians' Continuing Ineptitude

Both the PA and Hamas are foolishly hoping that their lot will improve over time, which is only another illusion; instead of addressing the people's needs, each political faction is competing to unseat the other. To be sure, the Palestinian leadership, moderate and extremist alike, has failed its people time and again and missed many opportunities to end the conflict with Israel, using the people as pawns in their game of brinkmanship to outdo one another for both public consumption and in their position toward Israel.[8] Tragically, Palestinian leaders have still learned nothing from their dismal failures over several decades.

Their most recent failure was their reaction to the Abraham Accords between Israel and the UAE, Bahrain, Morocco, and Sudan, which has created a significantly more favorable climate to resume the peace negotiations. Instead of capitalizing on the Accords (which forbids Israel from further annexing any Palestinian territories) and signaling to Israel their willingness to restart peace negotiations unconditionally and eventually join the Abraham

---

8   The Palestinians with the support of the Arab states soundly rejected Israel's offer to surrender all captured territories in 1967 with the exception of Jerusalem in exchange for peace. Their rejection was formulated in Khartoum by passing a unanimous resolution, known for its three "no"s: no negotiations, no recognition, and no peace. The Palestinians rejected the late Egyptian President Anwar Sadat's invitation to join the peace negotiations in 1974. PA Chairman Arafat rebuffed a nearly complete peace agreement at Camp David in 2000 and several other missed opportunities to reach a peace agreement in between.

Accords, they condemned these historic agreements. Moreover, they have failed to grasp that the Abraham Accords allow the Arab states to exert greater political influence on Israel on behalf of the Palestinians, especially because Israel wants to expand the Accords to include other Arab states. The Palestinians could have taken full advantage of the new political environment between Israel and the Arab states that was created by the Accords, but instead, this has become yet another missed opportunity in a string of missed opportunities. Meanwhile, the Palestinian people continue to suffer under their inept leadership which is steadily losing its political and moral compass.

No wonder the Arab states have also grown weary of the Israeli-Palestinian conflict, and although they continue to support the Palestinians' quest for an independent state, they are now more focused on the threats to their own national security emanating from Iran, jihadist groups, and radical Islamists, such as the Shiite Hezbollah organization. They have come to view Israel as an asset rather than an adversary, one on whom they can count as being on the front line of defense to prevent Shiite Iran from realizing its ambition to become the region's hegemon. The normalization of relations under the Abraham Accords suggests a dramatic shift in the Arab states' priorities. Although they have not abandoned the Palestinian cause, they have become weary of the Palestinians being stuck in their dead-end position. As such, the Arab states saw no urgency in finding a solution to the conflict, just as long as *Israel does not annex more Palestinian territory*, the intermittent Israeli-Palestinian violence continues to be managed, and any major flareups are prevented.

The United States, which continues to be the most important interlocutor between Israel and the Palestinians and has made repeated efforts in the past three decades to mediate a solution to their conflict, has basically given up trying to find a peaceful solution. During his visit to the region from July 13-16, 2022, President Biden paid no more than lip service to the conflict, making it clear that the political environment between the two sides does not lend itself to undertaking any new peace initiative. Moreover, given the country's internal political strife since Trump rose to power in 2017, among a plethora of other domestic problems, in addition to tension with China, the protracted negotiations with Iran over its nuclear program, and Russia's war against Ukraine, it is highly unlikely that the Biden administration will seek to settle a problem as intractable as the Israeli-Palestinian conflict, above those other more urgent concerns and conflicts facing America.

Finally, the EU, which continues to engage the Israelis and Palestinians on many levels and, like the United States, has strong geostrategic interests in the region, finds itself at a loss and has made no headway over the last decade to advance the Israeli-Palestinian peace process. The EU has refrained from taking any new peace initiative in recent years, conceding to the prevailing notion that the time has not arrived for any bold peace offensive; instead, it has inadvertently settled for the status quo. Just like the United States, the EU has its own share of problems partly emanating from its long-winded wranglings over Brexit, worrying relations with the United States during the Trump administration, and continuing anxiety over the current political discourse in America. And presently they are preoccupied by the Russia-Ukraine war and its security implications, including the economic instability resulting from the disruption of energy supplies and future uncertainty. Given its immediate concerns, the EU resigned itself to the prevailing circumstances—a solution to the Israeli-Palestinian conflict can wait for another day.

The danger that all concerned parties seem to overlook is that although on the surface the status quo between Israel and the Palestinians may prevail for a little longer, say three-to-four years, it cannot be sustained for much beyond that. It is bound to explode in the face of everyone who does not realize the urgency and the dire consequences in the absence of a solution. Indeed, it is not a matter of if but when the Palestinians will rise and resort to violence, making the Second Intifada in 2000 look like a mere rehearsal. And the Israelis who have been living in denial will sooner rather than later have to face the bitter truth. The Palestinian problem will not go away; it will continue to haunt them and offer no respite. Moreover, the conflict with the Palestinians will continue to provide Israel's staunchest enemy, Iran, and its proxy Hezbollah in Lebanon, the perfect recipe they need to destabilize the region and constantly threaten Israel's national security. And whereas Israel can prevail militarily over any of its enemies, albeit at an increasing toll in blood and treasure, it cannot stop the most dangerous threat of all—the deadly erosion, resulting from its continuing brutal occupation, of that moral foundation on which the country was established.

The Palestinians, moderate and extremist alike, must also realize that Israel is here to stay, regardless of what they say, do, or plot. Their fate is intertwined with Israel. They can live and prosper, and feel safe and secure only if Israel feels the same. But as long as any segment of the Palestinian population—especially Hamas and Islamic Jihad, who do not represent the majority of the Palestinian population—poses a threat to Israel's existence, however illusory that may be, it will still provide Israel with the perfect excuse to maintain its siege and let the Palestinians continue to languish under occupation. By now the Palestinians must understand that after 55 years of occupation, Israel's entrenchment in the occupied territories has only deepened and continued violent resistance plays directly into the hands of right-wing Israelis who are becoming the majority and oppose the establishment of a Palestinian state. The Palestinians will do well to remember that, while the Arab states oppose the occupation and support the establishment of an independent Palestinian state, their normalization of relations with Israel is no longer contingent upon Israel's return of Palestinian territory. Their past unanimous support of the Palestinians has now given way to their immediate national security concerns and economic well-being.

THE MAJOR CONFLICTING ISSUES

Changing the dynamic of the conflict will require a close look from a humanitarian perspective at its major components—the fate of the Palestinian refugees, the occupation and interspersed Israeli and Palestinian populations, Jerusalem, and national security. These factors have shaped the nature of the conflict and created new conditions on the ground that *only the Israelis and Palestinians themselves can effectively address* with the support of the United States, EU, Saudi Arabia, Jordan, and Egypt.

Palestinian Refugees[9]

A resolution to the Palestinian refugee issue is one of the four central conflicting issues and no solution to the Israeli-Palestinian conflict can be found until this agonizing and troublesome issue is settled with definitive efficacy and execution. For more than seven decades, Palestinian leaders made the refugee problem front and center in the conflict with Israel, while methodically engaging in narratives that imbued the public with the notion that the Palestinian refugees' right of return is *sine qua non* to finding a peaceful solution.

From previous negotiations, going back to the mid-1990s, Israel made it abundantly clear (and the PA understood and conceded, albeit not publicly) that under no circumstances will Israel allow the return of any significant number of refugees—only at most a symbolic few thousand (perhaps 25,000 to 30,000) under family reunification. As Israel sees it, the return of the refugees would demographically obliterate the Jewish national character of the state, which is the raison d'etre behind Israel's creation.

Nevertheless, the problem is that Palestinian leaders have consistently and publicly been promoting the right of return, regardless of how illusory it may be. Palestinians from all political persuasions

---

9   From Alon Ben-Meir, "The Case for an Israeli-Palestinian-Jordanian Confederation: Why Now and How?" *World Affairs* 185, no. 1 (February 10, 2022): 9–58, https://doi.org/10.1177/00438200211066350.

continue to support the right of return because they see it as the glue that keeps all Palestinians "united." In fact, Palestinian leaders have consistently exploited the right of return, which became more of a slogan to rally the people around an emotional issue and make it the centerpiece of their own political agenda. Every Palestinian leader, starting with Yasser Arafat, knew only too well that they were misleading their public and that the right of return, as they described it, would never be realized.

It is time for the Palestinians to disabuse themselves of the notion of the right of return *as they currently envision it*. Instead, the Palestinians must redefine the right of return—not to the exact towns and villages (and in some claims, exact homes) from which they and their ancestors fled, but to a return to the State of Palestine in general, which is in line with the international legal principle of right of return, which grants this return to "one's own country." Indeed, only 29 percent of Palestinians see "the right of return to refugees to their 1948 towns and villages" as an important goal.[xxxii] Palestinian leaders only keep this as a goal to sustain their momentum, knowing it will never be fulfilled, and use it as a bargaining chip in future negotiations. The solution to the refugee issue rests then, as it always has, on compensation and/or resettlement, mostly in the West Bank and Gaza (in relatively smaller numbers), and offering compensation for those who choose not to relocate, be they in Lebanon, Syria, Jordan, or beyond.

Additionally, this is in line with UNGA Resolution 194 (1948), which stipulates that "refugees wishing to return to their homes and live at peace with their neighbors *should be permitted to do so at the earliest practicable date*, and that compensation *should be paid for the property* of those choosing not to return and for loss of or damage to property which, under principles of international law or equity, should be made good by the Governments or authorities responsible [emphasis added]," and which the PLO has long-cited as its basis for the right of return.[10]

---

10   This is also in line with proposals introduced at Camp David in 2000 and the

The funds for resettling and/or compensating the Palestinian refugees ought to be raised from the oil-rich Arab states as well as the US and the EU, all of which have the resources to provide the necessary funding for that purpose. Obviously, the total amount required will depend on how many Palestinian refugees want to relocate and settle in the West Bank and Gaza, and how many will seek compensation.[11] Based on current knowledge of the countries mentioned above, they will be ready to provide the bulk of the funds for that purpose, estimated by various sources to be roughly $10 billion, to be administered by representatives of the donor countries with the involvement of UNRWA.[xxxiii] This UN agency continues to spearhead the Palestinian refugee programs, as it has for the past seven decades. The agency keeps and maintains records of refugees—their population, movements, and places of residence.

Given the sensitivity of the refugee issue and the decades-long focus on the right of return, which sadly has been exploited for political gains by the Arab states and the Palestinian Authority in particular, the solution to this problem ought to begin at the onset of the process of reconciliation. There will be some resistance to that by Palestinian extremists, who have been using the right of return to rally the public behind their own agenda. However, once the funds become available, both the PA and Hamas will be hard-pressed not to oppose resettlement and/or compensation as they stand to benefit greatly from the funds infused for that purpose.

There are no means by which the Palestinians can compel Israel to concede the principle of the right of return. During the process of reconciliation, the Palestinian leadership must begin to tone down

---

subsequent Clinton parameters, and Olmert's peace offer in 2008.

11   According to a 2003 poll conducted by the Palestinian Center for Policy and Survey Research among Palestinian refugees residing in the West Bank, Gaza, Jordan, and Lebanon, 54 percent would choose to settle in the West Bank and Gaza, or designated areas of Israel that would be included in a land swap with Israel; 73 percent would seek compensation of some amount. Only 10 percent would seek Israeli citizenship and resettlement in Israel proper.

their demand on this issue in a sincere effort to gradually disabuse the public of the notion that the right of return is central to finding a permanent solution to the conflict with Israel.

The Israeli Settlements

The issue of the continued building and expansion of Israeli settlements in the West Bank resurfaced as the central contentious issue between the two sides, threatening to torpedo the peace process altogether. Israelis and the Palestinians view the settlements enterprise from completely different perspectives that define their strategic objectives, and the issue is becoming increasingly irreconcilable every time Israel announces the building of new housing units. As the Palestinians see it, the continued settlement activity and their very existence throughout the West Bank stand in total contradiction to their objective of an independent state on a contiguous landmass. Consequently, this will inevitably deprive them of establishing a state of their own on the same territory.

Since the Oslo signing of the Declaration of Principles in September 1993, the number of Israeli settlers in the West Bank has tripled, from 110,000 to approximately 465,000 today, plus approximately 230,000 settlers in East Jerusalem, where thousands of new housing units are continuously being built.[xxxiv] Physically, settlement construction confiscates land bit by painstaking bit and sends a clear message: Israel does not accept the Palestinians' claim to the land or their internationally recognized right to establish an independent state of their own.

The Palestinians insist that contrary to his public pronouncements, Prime Minister Netanyahu has no intention of pursuing a peace agreement based on a two-state solution. They point to his relentless efforts to expand the settlements by following the mantra of the late extreme rightist Prime Minister Yitzhak Shamir from the mid-to-late-1980s, who fiercely promoted the idea that Israel should settle "half a million" Jews in the West Bank, creating an irreversible fact that no one can change.[xxxv]

Although from early 2000, freezing construction was not a precondition to resuming negotiations, the problem for the Palestinian Authority is that the expansion of settlements during the negotiating process is seen by the public as caving in on the core issue, which discredits the whole purpose of the negotiations. Indeed, continued settlement activity made it extremely difficult politically for President Abbas to compromise on other critical issues for Israel, such as the right of return of the Palestinian refugees. This is particularly daunting for the Palestinians when seen in the context of Israel's refusal to compromise on the one issue that determines the future of Palestinian nationhood.

Netanyahu's position is that the settlements will not impede reaching a peace agreement with the Palestinians. How he plans to mitigate that with the reality on the ground, however, remains a mystery, specifically when his repeated public pronouncements about Israel's inherent right to the land point to the contrary. Prime Minister Netanyahu remains to this day adamant about Israel's right to maintain a considerable presence in the West Bank, justified from his perspective by several unadulterated facts:

First, Netanyahu insists that the Jews have a historical affinity to the entire "land of Israel" as envisioned by the Zionist movement. Unlike his predecessors, Ehud Olmert, Ariel Sharon and Ehud Barak, ideologically he does not view the West Bank as an occupied territory (which he refers to by its Hebrew name, Judea and Samaria). Thus, he maintains that the West Bank should not be off-limits to Jewish inhabitants.

Second, Netanyahu and many Israelis with strong religious convictions uphold the view that the land has been bequeathed to the Jews, who have a biblical birthright to live in it. Zealous settlers deeply believe they are pursuing God's mission and that the Almighty is testing their resolve, tenacity, and willingness to make any sacrifice before He grants them the Promised Land in perpetuity.

Third, Netanyahu has consistently linked the settlements to Israel's national security, which an increasing number of Israelis accept at face value. He has repeatedly claimed that Israel cannot accept "indefensible borders" based on the 1967 lines and highlights that Israel would be only nine miles wide if it were to relinquish much of its presence in the West Bank.

Fourth, the more practical motivation behind the settlements is the desire of many Israelis, with the government's encouragement, to live in affordable and spacious housing in a clean environment with easy access to urban centers. To attract more settlers, successive governments have subsidized housing, schools, security, and other services.

As a consequence, the four factors led to the expansion of the settlements and the rise of the settlement movement as a formidable political force fully entrenched in the body politic of the country. Over time, it has acquired a near *de facto* veto power over policies affecting the future disposition of the West Bank. Indeed, the settler movement is not a small group of criminals and vandals who are out to burn or daub inflammatory graffiti on the walls of Palestinian mosques or vandalize Israeli military bases, although many such incidents have occurred. This is a movement on which successive coalition governments came to rely on to engender wide political support.

If the dispute over settlements was solely based on security or political issues, it could be reconciled through good-faith negotiations and iron-clad security guarantees. However, the settlements represent more than a security and political disagreement. All of this begs the question: will the Netanyahu government or any extremist right-wing one recognize that its policy on the settlements has set the stage for further escalation of violent confrontations? The United Nations and many major powers, including the US and the EU member states, consider the settlements to be "illegitimate" and a violation of international law.

What is needed here are fundamental policy changes that must first, cease construction of new and legalization of illegal settlements and second, commit in deeds, rather than empty rhetoric, to a two-state solution. Otherwise, the Netanyahu government runs the risk of the settlements becoming a self-consuming cancer. Moreover, continued settlement construction will increase the divide between Israelis who seek an end to the conflict with the Palestinians and hard-core ideologues like Netanyahu, who deny the evidence that the settlements burden ordinary Israelis who are paying for it through cost of living and lack of affordable housing. Religiously committed Israelis, on the other hand, need no evidence to justify their convictions as they place the building and expansion of settlements as the singular historic opportunity that will restore Jewish birthright to their homeland.

The uprooting of a significant number of settlers will indeed be the most divisive issue that will face Israel. But then, no solution to the Israeli-Palestinian conflict is possible without relocating some of the 468,000 settlers scattered across the West Bank.

Some Israelis living in small settlements scattered throughout the West Bank (consisting of 43 settlements in which more than 214,000 settlers reside)[12] can be relocated to larger ones, albeit some of them will resist. But if the Israeli government provides them with better or equal housing, job opportunities, and some financial incentives, they would relocate peacefully. The vast majority of settlers, however, will stay in place because no Israeli government, regardless of its political leaning, will agree to remove such settlements. As was agreed in previous peace negotiations in 2008–2009 and 2013–2014, the Palestinians will be compensated through land swaps (constituting approximately four to six percent of the territory) to make up for land used, especially by the three large settlement blocs along the 1967 border (commonly acknowledged as Ma'ale Adumim, Gush Etzion, and Betar Illit, although

---

12 All figures, unless otherwise cited, are courtesy of Hagit Ofran, Settlement Watch director for Peace Now, who I thank for sharing her statistics on the settlements.

the exact configuration is still open for debate). All in all, these settlements included in land swaps will encompass approximately 80 percent of all Israeli settlers.[xxxvi]

There will still be other settlements, such as Ariel, which will undoubtedly remain on Palestinian-controlled land. The Palestinians have no choice but to accept that hundreds of thousands of Israelis will continue to live in settlements in the West Bank, and the Palestinian Authority's demand to remove all settlements outside the three blocs is a non-starter.[13] However, the residents of many of the smaller settlements will have to be relocated perhaps to the larger three blocks of settlements in order to create land contiguity for the future Palestinian state.

Interspersed Populations

The fact that the Israelis and Palestinians are interspersed in the West Bank, Jerusalem, and Israel proper and *anchored in their current places of residence* makes it simply impossible to physically separate them or relocate a large segment of either population. There are an estimated 2.7 million Palestinians and 468,000 Israelis in the West Bank,[14] and in East Jerusalem, there are nearly 361,700 Palestinians and 233,700 Israelis who mostly live in the post-1967 Jewish neighborhoods surrounding East Jerusalem, which the Palestinians consider settlements.[xxxvii] There are also roughly 1.9 million Israeli Arab citizens, and while their status is dissimilar to the settlers living in the West Bank, the fact that they live in their country—Israel—as full-fledged citizens suggests that cohabitation of Israelis and Palestinians is inescapable. It should be noted that notwithstanding the fact that Israeli Arabs are citizens of Israel, they certainly have a deep affinity toward their brethren in the territories, which adds a social and cultural component to the intersper-

---

13 As it stands, the three settlement blocs mentioned encompass 80 percent of all Jewish settlers in the West Bank; the remaining settlements apart from Ariel (which has a stagnant population) are individually very small and make up only 20 percent of the entire settler population.

14 Demographic figures from *The World Factbook* unless otherwise noted.

sion of the two populations. The Palestinians in the West Bank are gradually coming to terms with the fact that Israeli Jews living in their midst is *also an irreversible reality.*

The interspersion of Israelis and Palestinians in the West Bank and in Jerusalem is a permanent factor that has three dimensions. First, it will be impossible to erect a hard border between the two sides, as there will always be Israelis and Palestinians living in each other's territory who will want to move freely across the boundary. Jerusalem offers a good example where Israelis and Palestinians are able to mingle and enjoy freedom of movement between the East and West sides of the city.

Second, since uprooting Israelis or Palestinians in the hundreds of thousands from their current places of residence is impossible, there will be a need for extensive collaboration in relation to security and economic development, which will render the current hard border over time simply a political line.

Third, people and goods must be able to move freely in both directions, which in any case is necessitated by their respective populations' close proximity. However, this free movement does not infringe on their mutual independence but will expand the level of cooperation on many other levels.

Under such a scenario, there will be a need to differentiate between citizenship and permanent residency. Israelis living in the West Bank can vote or be elected in Israel while maintaining permanent residency in the West Bank, provided they adhere to local laws and ordinances. The same is applicable to Palestinians, especially those living in East Jerusalem. (This is not applicable to Israeli Arabs, who are Israeli citizens who can vote and be elected in the State of Israel.) To maintain the Jewish national identity of Israel and that of Palestine, relinquishing citizenship for the other will be allowed only on rare occasions, such as when intermarriage occurs.

If Israel wants to maintain its democracy and its Jewish national identity, there is no other viable formula that can sustain that. To suggest that Israel can uphold the military occupation with different sets of laws and rules for Palestinians and Jewish Israelis is an illusion. The Palestinians will never give up their right to a state of their own regardless of how benevolent the Israeli government may be, especially because they continue to enjoy the overwhelming support of the international community.

Some Israelis and an increasing number of Palestinians have concluded that the only solution to the conflict must now rest *on the creation of one state,* given the irreversible reality of the interspersed Israeli and Palestinian populations, especially in the West Bank and Jerusalem. Whereas on the surface this may seem to be the most practical solution, there are no circumstances under which Israel would agree to such an outcome, as it would defy the very reason behind the creation of the State of Israel in the first place. The founders of Israel envisioned a Jewish and democratic state that would offer a refuge to all Jews as the answer for ending millennia-old persecution, discrimination, and expulsion culminating with the near-destruction of all European Jewry during World War II. However, under no one-state scenario would both Israel's democracy and Jewish identity be preserved. For this reason, no Israeli government has ever and will never seriously entertain the idea of a one-state solution.

The 2.7 million Palestinians in the West Bank and the 1.9 million Israeli Arabs will constitute roughly 45 percent of the total combined population of Jewish and Arab Israelis and Palestinians. If we were to include the Palestinians in Gaza, the total number of Palestinians and Israeli Arabs will be near that of Israeli Jews. Although the Jewish fertility rate has now surpassed that of the Arabs for the first time, with an average 3.1 per Jewish woman versus 3 per Israeli-Arab woman,[15] that does not change by much the demographic time bomb.[xxxviii] In fact, even without the Palestinians in Gaza, a minority of nearly 50 percent makes it impossible to maintain the

---

15 Among Palestinians, the fertility rate is 3.8 in the West Bank and 3.9 in Gaza.

Jewish national character of Israel without violating the Palestinians' human and political rights.

The projected demographic growth of both communities clearly shows that the Palestinians would become the ruling majority within less than a decade. As is, in 2021, Israel could not form a new government following three rounds of elections without inviting one Israeli Arab party to join the coalition government. If Israel were to preserve its democracy and grant every Israeli and Palestinian the right to vote, it would obliterate the Jewish national identity of the state, which the vast majority of Jews in Israel refuse to allow. If Israel instead chose to protect its Jewish national identity and rejected suffrage for Palestinians under one state, it would then unequivocally become an apartheid state.

A relative majority of Israelis want to indefinitely control the West Bank, if not outright annex most of it and prevent the establishment of a Palestinian state, and plan to maintain the status quo by continuing to employ two sets of laws. Israeli Jews living in the West Bank are full-fledged Israeli citizens and are governed by Israeli laws, while Palestinians in the West Bank are governed by military rules with all the restrictions that entails, including restriction of civil rights and freedom of movement, detentions, and arbitrary searches and seizures, among others.

Former Israeli Prime Minister Naftali Bennett, who openly and resolutely opposes the creation of a Palestinian state and wants to keep the Palestinians at bay, had taken various measures to make the occupation decreasingly oppressive, hoping that the Palestinians will eventually settle for the status quo and accept their lot under a more "benevolent" occupation. This type of "one state" solution, which Netanyahu and his right-wing partners want to perpetuate, is unrealistic. Many Palestinians will accept a one state solution only if they are given the same rights as Israeli Jews under a democratic form of government, knowing that they will end up being the governing authority over a period of a few years, which is a complete non-starter for the vast majority of Israelis.

To be sure, the interspersion of Israelis and Palestinians is a reality that cannot be wished away. Since uprooting any significant number of Israelis or Palestinians from their current places of residence is unacceptable by either side and in fact impossible, *only a confederation would allow for continuing the current interspersion of the populations while preserving the independence of Israeli and Palestinian states.*

Jerusalem

Jerusalem is unique in that both Israelis and Palestinians—and many Jews, Muslims, and Christians around the world—have a special affinity to the city. Three major factors attest to the city's uniqueness and hence the necessity of full collaboration between the three member states.

First, East Jerusalem houses the largest mixed Jewish-Arab community in the world, with roughly 361,700 Arabs and 233,700 Israelis.[xxxix] Although the majority of Palestinians live in East Jerusalem, they move freely across the city east and west and throughout Israel. Israelis and Palestinians mingle and transact regularly throughout the city, and neither side expects that to change under any peace agreement.

Second, the city's infrastructure and services—roads, electrical grid, communication, and maintenance—are all fully integrated. There is simply no way that these services and the interconnectedness between the two sides can be altered significantly. In fact, neither Israel nor the Palestinians want to physically divide the city, regardless of its final political status.

Third, Jerusalem is home to the Jews' holiest shrine, the Western Wall (the outer wall of the Second Temple), the third-holiest Muslim shrines, the al-Aqsa Mosque and the Dome of the Rock (Haram al-Sharif), and the holiest sites in Christianity within the Church of the Holy Sepulchre. All three Abrahamic religions respect each other's religious affinity to the city. The fact that the

Jewish and Arab holy shrines are adjacent to one another, and no physical change can take place, suggests that there will always be the need to fully collaborate on security, tourism, access, and improvements to all of the holy sites, and no side will be allowed, under any circumstances, to make any physical change that will alter the current status quo.

Whereas Israel claims that all of Jerusalem, East and West, is the capital of Israel based on biblical and historical claims, the Palestinians also have religious claims based on the Quranic "Night Journey," when the Prophet Mohammed stopped in Jerusalem on his way to heaven, and insist that East Jerusalem must be the capital of their future state. However, given that the city under any circumstances will remain united physically, and that the majority of the population in the old section of East Jerusalem is Palestinian, it stands to reason in practical terms as well that the Palestinians should have a say about the administration of East Jerusalem.

Under any future framework for peace, East and West Jerusalem would have independent municipalities with their own administrative prerogatives. East Jerusalem would be the capital of the Palestinian state, and West Jerusalem would be the capital of Israel, and a joint Israeli-Palestinian commission covering the entirety of Jerusalem would be established to handle any issues or services that impact the two sections of the city. This includes electricity, water, and other municipal services, cross-border crimes, and development projects that affect both sides of the city, to name a few examples.

The commission should operate based on advice and consent by the members of the commission. The chairman of the commission should alternate between an Israeli and a Palestinian for a period to be mutually agreed upon. Such commissioners should have special expertise on issues of importance to the city, including law enforcement, civil engineering, public health, and transportation, among others. The number of commissioners and their expressed duties and responsibilities will be established by mutual consent. The commission will have a clear and well-defined mandate to ensure *that neither side can infringe on the other's separate municipal independence and responsibilities.*

In this regard, since Israel occupied East Jerusalem in 1967, the Hashemite Kingdom of Jordan has and continues to maintain the custodianship and the administration of the Muslim holy shrines, Haram al-Sharif. Jordan will continue to administer the Muslim shrines, while Israel will continue to maintain its control over the Western Wall. That is, under any circumstances, the three sides will have to cooperate and work closely to ensure the security and future development of these sites, including excavation without prejudice of their respective shrines. As part of this, a religious council encompassing Judaism, Islam, and Christianity would be established to deal with various issues related to their religious dominion over their holy shrines.

Israel will have to accept that the Palestinians will establish their capital in East Jerusalem, *while all Israeli Jews living on the east side of the city will remain in place.* In fact, the Trump administration's official recognition of Jerusalem as Israel's capital clearly states that "We are not taking a position on any final status issues, including the specific boundaries of the Israeli sovereignty in Jerusalem, or the resolution of contested borders. Those questions are up to the parties involved."[xl]

A majority of Israelis insist that Israel will never give up its sovereignty over East Jerusalem, be that for biblical or historical reasons.[16] They argue that the Palestinians' future capital should be established in either Abu Dis, on the outskirts of Jerusalem, or Silwan, which would be incorporated into Greater Jerusalem. The Palestinians have rejected these proposals off-hand and are unlikely to abandon their quest of making East Jerusalem the capital of

---

16   However, a majority of such Israelis making biblical or historic claims also do not consider most of the 18 Palestinian villages that were incorporated into the city after 1967 an integral part of Jerusalem.

their future state, especially because they have the backing of the Arab states. In fact, despite the normalization agreements between Israel and various Arab countries, the Arab states continue to insist that the capital of the Palestinian state should be East Jerusalem, which must become an integral part of the Palestinian state. Jerusalem serves as an extremely important symbol to the Arab world as a whole. That said, the city will remain totally open for both Israelis and Palestinians to move freely in both directions, which is in essence a continuation of the current status quo.

Given the fact that Jerusalem is the home of the largest mixed Jewish-Palestinian community, and since the city will remain united under any circumstances, Jerusalem will become a microcosm of Israeli-Palestinian coexistence. It has been such since Israel captured East Jerusalem in 1967. Thus, if peaceful coexistence is a must in Jerusalem, it can certainly be applicable in the West Bank, even in the case of Hebron, where the small number of settlers (like all others that will not be transferred to Israel proper) will abide under local laws, albeit with some tension, which will certainly recede in due course *under conditions of peace.*

National Security[17]

For obvious reasons, Israel's national security and the Palestinians' sense of insecurity are sources of great concern to both sides, particularly as they are directly connected. Therefore, security collaboration is central to any peace agreement. Even now, there is extensive security collaboration, such as intelligence sharing, apprehending would-be terrorists, and coordination between security forces. There are many Israelis who believe that regardless of the contours of a mutually-agreed border, current security arrangements, and even those in the future, the Palestinians will still fight to regain all of the land, from the Mediterranean Sea to the Jordan River. Even if this were to be true, by what means, military or

---

17 From Alon Ben-Meir, "The Case for an Israeli-Palestinian-Jordanian Confederation: Why Now and How?"

otherwise, can they, in reality, push Israel out of existence? Those Israelis who do not want to relinquish the occupation of the West Bank often use national security as the rationale behind their persistent opposition to the creation of a Palestinian state, albeit any peace agreement must be based on a solid security collaboration between the two sides.

It is critically important for the Palestinians to understand that notwithstanding the fact that Israel is the most powerful country in the region by virtue of its formidable military strength and operational nuclear capability (thus with an ability to confront almost any threat), the Israelis still experience a sense of existential vulnerability. This is traceable to the Jews' historical experiences as a scapegoat and persecuted minority throughout Europe, the Middle East, and North Africa. The systematic persecution of the Jews, especially in Europe, which culminated in the Holocaust, where six million Jews were murdered, left an indelible mark on every Jew, and they are still haunted by that unimaginable calamity to this day.

Thus, the concern over Israel's national security is psychologically ingrained, and neither its own military prowess nor external assurances to protect its security, including from the US, completely assuage those concerns. For this reason, Israel takes very seriously the fact that there is a considerable segment of the Palestinian population, in particular Hamas and Islamic Jihad, which still threatens Israel's very existence.[18] Regardless of how real or exaggerated such threats may be, it makes little difference because Israel takes nothing for granted where its national security is concerned.

The Palestinians' initial rejection, along with the Arab states, of the establishment of a Jewish state, and extremist Palestinians' continuing existential threats, reinforced Israel's national security concerns. In many ways, the Second Intifada in 2000 was a turning point for most Israelis as it erupted immediately following the

---

18   While Hamas' public posture seeks the destruction of Israel, privately Hamas leaders admit that Israel is there to stay.

failed peace negotiations at Camp David, which Israel conducted in good faith, and where the establishment of a Palestinian state was treated as a given. This gave rise to the notion among a multitude of Israelis that the Palestinians *can never be trusted and their ultimate aim is to liquidate Israel, and hence,* they ought to be permanently subjugated and treated with an iron fist. On the contrary, it is neither logical nor practical for any government of an independent Palestinian state to allow any extremist individuals or groups to threaten Israel. They know full well that Israel can enter the West Bank at will and impose new harsh restrictions that would severely compromise the country's independence. This is a likely outcome that no Palestinian government would ever want to occur, as once the Palestinians have their independence, they will not want to do anything to compromise that—which works entirely in Israel's favor from a security perspective.

What the Israelis fail to understand, however, is that their drive to achieve absolute security rendered the Palestinians absolutely insecure. In the wake of the First Intifada beginning in 1987, Israel pursued harsh policies toward the Palestinians prompted by their own sense of insecurity, which intensified greatly after the Second Intifada. As a result, Israel engaged in security activities that resulted in human rights violations, which made the Palestinians feel ever more oppressed, humiliated, and vulnerable. Such violations included night raids against suspected Palestinian terrorists, unjustified incarcerations for months and even years without trial, restriction of movement, home demolitions, uprooting of olive groves by radical settlers, and creeping annexation of Palestinian territories to make room for the expansion of settlements.

The Israelis still justify these and other violations in the name of national security, when in fact it has become increasingly clear that successive Israeli governments were pursuing a policy of territorial expansionism by building more settlements throughout the West Bank. This policy, of course, exacerbated the Palestinians' distrust of the Israelis and deepened their conviction that Israel will not

ALON BEN-MEIR

allow the creation of a Palestinian state. Statements to that effect
were made explicitly on a number of occasions by Prime Minister
Netanyahu and openly expressed by the former Prime Minister,
Naftali Bennett.[19] Bennett not only opposes the establishment of
a Palestinian state, he has previously called for the annexation of
Area C in the West Bank, which comprises 60 percent of the entire
Palestinian territory.[xli]

One central security issue is the protection of the Jordan Valley.
While Israel insists on maintaining its own security forces along
the Jordan River, the Palestinians have rejected this as they consider the Jordan Valley an integral part of a future Palestinian state.
Given that Jordan's national security is intertwined with Israel, the
solution to the security of the Jordan Valley will rest on full collaboration between the three states. To be sure, Israel will insist on
such an arrangement, and there is no evidence that either the Palestinians or Jordan will categorically object to that. Such an arrangement would prevent the infiltration of terrorists and the smuggling
of weapons, and guard the broader external borders from threats
coming from Syria, Hezbollah, and Iran, which are of great concern
to Israel and Jordan, as well as to the Palestinians.

Collaboration on all security matters is essential; Israel will be
hard-pressed to make any significant concessions unless it is satis-
fied that its national security is not being compromised. The Palestinians, on the other hand, will retain sovereignty over the Jordan
Valley while benefitting from Israel's enhanced sense of security if
they take all security measures seriously and cease their threats because the safer Israel feels, the more lenient and accommodating it
will become.

---

19 When asked by former Israeli news site *NRG* in 2015 if there would be no
Palestinian state if he were prime minister, Netanyahu responded "Indeed."
Naftali Bennett as recently as January 2020 stated "…we will apply [Israeli]
sovereignty to all of Area C, not just the settlements…," albeit since becoming
Prime Minister he has stated that there will be no change in the territorial
status quo under his current government (Breitman 2015; Lazaroff 2020;
Kampeas 2021).

64

The newly-established Palestinian state must be demilitarized. The Palestinians do not need any military forces for three reasons: first, there is no regional enemy that will threaten the Palestinian state, especially once the Israeli-Palestinian-Jordanian confederation is established. Second, regardless of how powerful such a Palestinian military might be, it will never be in a position to overwhelm the Israeli military, as Israel will always maintain a military edge in the region that no enemy or a combination of enemies can overwhelm. Third, the Palestinians do not have the financial means to recruit and equip a military, regardless of how small it may be. Furthermore, Palestinian Authority President Mahmoud Abbas has on a number of occasions supported the demilitarization of a future Palestinian state, with its security managed by American-led NATO forces indefinitely.[xlii] However, the Palestinian state would retain its existing paramilitary security forces and handle any external threat jointly with Israel's and Jordan's militaries.

To that end, the future Palestinian state would significantly augment its domestic security apparatus and work very closely with Israel to prevent extremists from either side from committing acts of violence against the other. Their cooperation should include sharing intelligence, conducting joint operations to prevent violent attacks by individuals or groups from either side, and establishing rules of engagement to prevent accidental clashes between their respective security forces.

Finally, those Israelis who want to maintain the occupation often invoke what happened in Gaza following Israel's withdrawal in 2005. They argue that once the Palestinians assume total control of the West Bank, they will follow Hamas's footsteps and threaten Israel's urban centers with missiles and rockets and wreak havoc on the Israeli population. However, this argument is extremely misleading. Unlike the Israeli withdrawal from Gaza, which was done in haste and without any security arrangement or even agreement with the Palestinian Authority, which governed Gaza at the time, *Israel will not end the occupation of the West Bank without an iron-*

clad security arrangement with the PA. Moreover, the withdrawal of Israeli forces should be conducted in parallel with a process of reconciliation for a number of years to build bridges in all fields of life and mitigate the existing mistrust and hatred between the two sides. As mentioned above, and unlike the situation that prevailed in Gaza, there is already considerable security collaboration between Israel and the PA, which will only further expand under the framework of Israeli-Palestinian peace.

THE HORRIFIC BREAKDOWN IN ISRAELI-PALESTINIAN RELATIONS: WHERE DO WE GO FROM HERE?

The unprecedented and unfathomable savagery that Hamas inflicted on 1,200 innocent Israeli civilians and off-duty soldiers[xliii] has shaken to the core every human being with a conscience. Beyond that, it has also rattled the prevailing conditions between Israel and the Palestinians, making it impossible to return to the status quo ante. This incomprehensible massacre offers, though under horrifying circumstances, an unprecedented opportunity to bring a gradual end to the Israeli-Palestinian conflict. Those Israeli and Palestinian extremists who have been dismissive of each other's right to exist in an independent state and in peace have now been awakened to the bitterest reality—that both sides are here to stay.

This unparalleled breakdown resulting from Hamas's savagery has fundamentally changed the dynamic of the conflict and created a new paradigm that could lead to a breakthrough of historic proportions to reach a peace agreement based on a two-state solution. This opportunity can be realized or lost depending on how well thought-out the post-war strategic plans that Israel (and its indispensable ally, the US) put in place are, *which is of paramount importance,* and without which the sacrifices and losses that innocent Israelis and Palestinians have sustained will be in vain. And once again, it will be only a question of not if but when the next horrific Israeli-Palestinian conflagration will befall.

Since the 1967 Six Day War, many efforts have been made to reach a peace agreement between Israel and the Palestinians through *mediation* conducted by an impartial mediator, face-to-face *negotiations,* international conferences, offering *incentives, back-channel talks, interim agreements* (in particular, the Oslo Accords), and occasionally by an influential party exerting pressure on both sides, especially the US. As we know, none of the above approaches nor several others to reach a peace agreement have worked. The failures to reach an agreement are fundamentally attributed to the psychological impediments and how that impacted both sides' claims to exclusive ownership of the entire land from the Mediterranean to the Jordan River, albeit they blame each other for failing to make the necessary concessions to reach a peace agreement.

While the prospect of a two-state solution was viable following the 1993 Oslo Accords, the outlook for such a solution became progressively dimmer as Israel moved to the right-of-center. Prime Minister Netanyahu, who was bent on sabotaging the Oslo Accords when he served as prime minister between 1996 and 1999 and who has been in power for most of the past 15 years, made it clear repeatedly that there will be no Palestinian state under his watch. The idea of a two-state solution was steadily losing traction in Israel, the occupation of the West Bank was normalized, and a *de facto* apartheid state was created, which became a way of life for most Israelis and Palestinians.

The Changing Dynamic of the Conflict

It is well known in conflict resolution that sometimes it takes a major breakdown that precipitates an extraordinary crisis to change the dynamic of a conflict. The shockingly unexpected and devastating Yom Kippur War in 1973, which subsequently led to a peace agreement between Egypt and Israel, offers a potent example. As such, it made it simply *impossible to return to the status quo ante*. Indeed, neither Israel nor the Palestinians, including Hamas, will be the same following this most heinous and unprecedented massacre and Israel's retaliation that has already exacted (as of this writing) more than 30,000 Palestinian casualties[xliv]—not to speak of the unimaginable death and destruction that will still occur before the war comes to an end.

This unfolding horror should have been expected because of what was happening on the ground in the West Bank and Gaza over the past few years, especially in the last 15 months since the formation of the most extremist right-wing messianic coalition government in Israel's history (as I pointed out in my article published on October 3, 2022).[20] Indeed, it did not take a prophet to augur what would happen next. The increasingly violent flareups in the West Bank have been claiming hundreds of Palestinian lives, mostly under the age of 30, each year. In 2023, more than 500 Palestinians in the West Bank were killed, and since the beginning of 2024, nearly 50 have died as a result of the continuing violence.[xlv] Israel's frequent night raids, evictions, incarcerations, demolition of houses, and gross human rights abuses became the norm.

Despair, depression, and hopelessness swept much of the Palestinian population, akin to the gathering of a ferocious storm that successive Israeli governments led by Netanyahu chose to brush off. Moreover, it is *the psychological dimension of the conflict* that has now come into full display.

The Palestinians' resentment and hatred of Israel were intensifying. Since the new government could not formally annex Palestinian territories, it has resorted to intimidation and harassment of the Palestinians under the watchful eye of the criminal Minister of National Security, Itamar Ben-Gvir, who gave the settlers free reign to rampage Palestinian communities in order to "encourage" them to leave. The Netanyahu government's intent to slowly annex much of the West Bank became abundantly clear. None of the above can justify under any circumstances Hamas' heinous attack on Israeli civilians. Hamas must pay for it dearly. But such unthinkable carnage happened because of the perilous "strategy" that successive Israeli governments pursued that enabled Hamas and prevented the establishment of an independent Palestinian state. This also explains why Netanyahu consistently refused to negotiate with any prospective unity government between the PA and Hamas.

---

20 See Alon Ben-Meir, "Introduction to the Special Issue: Continued Israeli Occupation Is a Ticking Time Bomb," *World Affairs* 185, no. 4 (October 3, 2022): 650–75, https://doi.org/10.1177/00438200221128788.

The Creation of Hamas

Israel created Hamas to counterbalance the secular national PLO movement led by Yasser Arafat, which was intended to divide the Palestinians into two camps and prevent the creation of a Palestinian state. The creation of Hamas by Israel, which has been confirmed by many top Israeli military and civilian officials over a number of years, is unquestionable. Former Brig. Gen. Yitzhak Segev, who was the Israeli military governor in Gaza in the early 1980s, told a *New York Times* reporter that he had helped finance Hamas as a "counterweight" to the secularists and leftists of the PLO and the Fatah party, led by Yasser Arafat, stating "The Israeli Government gave me a budget and the military government gives to the mosques."[xlvi] And among many others, Avner Cohen, a former Israeli religious affairs official who worked in Gaza for more than two decades, told *The Wall Street Journal* in 2009 that *"Hamas, to my great regret, is Israel's creation."*[xlvii]

In a 2015 interview, Bezalel Smotrich, the current finance minister who is also in charge of Coordination of Government Activities in the Territories (COGAT), stated, "The Palestinian Authority is a burden, *and Hamas is an asset* [emphasis added]."[xlviii] In an article published in *The New York Times* on October 18, 2023, entitled "Netanyahu Led Us to Catastrophe. He Must Go," author Gershom Gorenberg stated that "Bringing Gaza back under the Palestinian Authority was apparently never part of the prime minister's agenda. Hamas was the enemy and, in a bizarre twist, an ally against the threat of diplomacy, a two-state solution and peace."[xlix]

Indeed, no Israeli prime minister has pursued this disastrous policy of divide and conquer more vigorously than Netanyahu. Although he maintained the blockade over Gaza, he allowed the flow of hundreds of millions of dollars from Qatar and other countries into Hamas' coffers, knowing full well that more than 50 percent of these funds were used by Hamas to buy and manufacture weapons, including tens of thousands of rockets, and build a massive network of tunnels (between 350 to 450 miles long)[l] with command and control while readying itself for the next war.

Gorenberg further stated that "In 2019, for instance, Netanyahu explained why he allowed the Hamas regime in Gaza to be propped up with cash from Qatar rather than have it depend on a financial umbilical cord to the West Bank. He told Likud lawmakers that 'whoever is against a Palestinian state should be for' the Qatari funding..."[li] Yuval Diskin, head of Shin Bet from 2005–2011, stated in January 2013 that "If we look at it over the years, one of the main people contributing to Hamas's strengthening has been Bibi Netanyahu, since his first term as prime minister."[lii] And in a more telling statement from someone who has been deeply immersed in Israeli politics and governance, Ehud Barak stated in August 2019, "His [Netanyahu's] strategy is to keep Hamas alive and kicking … even at the price of abandoning the citizens [of the south] … in order to weaken the PA in Ramallah ...."[liii]

Netanyahu's ill-fated "strategy" was an illusion. He believed that he could control the monster that he nurtured over the years, which instead came back to slaughter hundreds of innocent Israelis who have been relying on their government for protection and were tragically let down. They have been betrayed by a prime minister who has been fixated on bolstering Israel's security in the West Bank while weakening the security of the southern front along the Gaza border. And while Netanyahu was sparing no effort to "reform" the judiciary, Hamas was planning, training, acquiring weapons, and perfecting the technique to wage the most daring assault against Israel that no one could have possibly imagined.

It all happened under Netanyahu's watch. And worse yet, how is it possible that the world's most renowned intelligence agency, Israel's Mossad, failed to detect the planning of an attack of such magnitude that it took perhaps more than a year to prepare? And why did Netanyahu ignore the warning of Egypt's Intelligence Minister General Abbas Kamel, who personally called Netanyahu and warned him that Hamas was likely to do "something unusual, a terrible operation" only 10 days before the attack?[liv]

I do not imply that Netanyahu knew what was going to happen and chose to ignore it, but rather that he was dismissive of what Hamas is capable of and believed that he had a good handle on what was happening in Gaza. He was preoccupied with passing legislation that would subordinate the Supreme Court and the appointment of judges to elected politicians, which would have destroyed Israel's democracy and allowed him to assume authoritarian powers, to which he insatiably aspired.

Although most Palestinians, be they in the West Bank or Gaza, are innocent civilians, the extremists among them have committed many egregious acts of violence against Israel. The Palestinian leaders missed many opportunities to make peace and made countless mistakes that aggravated their own situation. Moreover, by threatening Israel's very existence, extremist groups such as Hamas and Islamic Jihad allowed successive Israeli governments to make a strong case against the Palestinians by portraying them as an irredeemable mortal enemy that poses the greatest danger to Israel's national security and hence, the Palestinians cannot be a party to peace. With these perspectives established by the Israeli government, maintaining the occupation became the state policy, however unsustainable it has been deemed by any keen and informed observer.

The Israel-Hamas war

There is a general consensus that when the Israel-Hamas war is concluded, most of Hamas' political leaders will survive, and certainly a residual group of fighters will continue to resist, albeit Hamas will not be able to reconstitute itself and rule Gaza again, nor will Israel withdraw from Gaza without ascertaining that Hamas will not be in power. A transitional period of 12 months should follow, during which four fundamental conditions must be established:

1. An international peacekeeping force to keep the peace and prevent the smuggling of weapons into Gaza.[21] The composition of the peacekeeping force will include foreign powers such as the US, Canada, and some EU member states such as Spain and Ireland, as well as two to three Arab states, perhaps Algeria and Morocco, who are willing to join such a force.

2. A joint EU-Arab League interim authority to be in charge of restoring normalcy by aiding the internally displaced and beginning the arduous tasks of clearing and rebuilding infrastructure and housing. Governance will be through an interim Palestinian Authority administration.

3. Preparation of the Palestinians in the West Bank and Gaza for general elections to be monitored by a commission of independent observers, which could include representatives from the Arab League, Council of Europe, and the Organization for Security and Co-operation in Europe (OSCE, whose members include the United States), and other international and domestic NGO monitoring groups.

4. Gradual withdrawal of Israeli forces once the peacekeeping force is in place and is functioning and in full control, and once a new Palestinian Authority takes charge.[22]

The Israeli Naysayers

Prime Minister Netanyahu and his right-wing followers, who insist that Israel should maintain overall security over Gaza indefinitely or even rebuild Jewish settlements, seem to have learned nothing from 57 years of occupation and the never-ending violence that culminated with Hamas' grisly attack. Reoccupying Gaza in full or in part in addition to the West Bank is perilous and a nonstarter,

---

21 See https://peacekeeping.un.org/en/terminology for the full peacekeeping terminology.

22 For further details, see "Israel-Hamas War Affirms the Indispensability Of A Two-State Solution," https://www.pressenza.com/2023/12/israel-hamas-war-affirms-the-indispensability-of-a-two-state-solution/.

as is maintaining the blockade. Certainly, Israel cannot expel the Palestinians, and *the US can prevent Israel by the many means at its disposal*, including political pressure, halting the supply of certain weapons, and withholding economic aid, from pursuing such an ill-fated and explosive path.

Whereas the vast majority of Israelis are calling for new elections to oust Netanyahu and his culprits (only fifteen percent want him to remain prime minister after the war),[lv] a relative majority (55 percent) oppose the establishment of a Palestinian state,[lvi] especially at this juncture when they are still deeply traumatized by the tragedy of October 7. They need to be convinced that their future security will be enhanced by the creation of a Palestinian state; without it, Israel's security will otherwise be constantly compromised. The bloodshed and destruction of 57 years of occupation provide the ultimate proof that the occupation has rendered the Israelis insecure. Netanyahu spuriously and successfully brainwashed the Israelis to believe that sustaining the occupation was critical to Israel's national security and that he *needed a perpetual enemy* to validate his blatant deceptiveness. His false claim did nothing but further harden the Palestinians' resolve to rid themselves of the occupation by whatever means available, which has become increasingly fatal over the years, as attested by the horrific Israel-Hamas war.

Based on my regular review of the Israeli political scene and public sentiment, *offering such a framework publicly* will dramatically change the political landscape in Israel. Under the current political and security atmosphere, a majority of Israelis (51 percent) responded in a January 2024 poll that they would be open to the establishment of a demilitarized Palestinian state in the West Bank and Gaza under an agreement that includes the return of the hostages and normalization with Saudi Arabia.[lvii] This real prospect of normalizing relations with the Arab states, particularly Saudi Arabia, will greatly resonate with the Israeli public and would unquestionably move the scale in favor of a new moderate government that supports a two-state solution.

New Israeli Elections

Since Netanyahu vehemently opposes the establishment of a Palestinian state, the prospect of creating it hinges on the political leaning and composition of the next Israeli government. Due to the fact that Netanyahu's popularity has sunk to a historic low, coupled with increasing public demand for a new general election even before the war ends, the current coalition government will be crushed if the election is held at the present. Repeated polls taken over the past several months show that the Netanyahu government will receive only 44 mandates (a record low of sixteen for Likud itself), compared to 71 for the opposition bloc, not including Gideon Saar's New Hope Party, which would bring an additional five seats to the bloc.[lviii]

A January Maariv poll asked, "If new elections were held for the Knesset today, who would you vote for?" The responses were: National Unity – 39 mandates, Likud – 16, Yesh Atid – 13, Yisrael Beiteinu – 10, Shas – 9, Otzma Yehudit – 9, United Torah Judaism – 6, New Hope – 5, Ra'am – 5, Meretz – 4, Religious Zionist Party – 4.[lix]

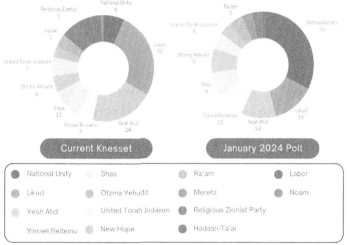

ISRAELI ELECTION POLLING

Current Knesset | January 2024 Poll

National Unity | Shas | Ra'am | Labor
Likud | Otzma Yehudit | Meretz | Noam
Yesh Atid | United Torah Judaism | Religious Zionist Party
Yisrael Beiteinu | New Hope | Hadash-Ta'al

Source: Jerusalem Post/Maariv January 2024 polling

Based on a careful review of this survey, a decisive majority of Israelis hold deep public disdain toward Netanyahu, and many *blame him directly for Hamas' daring onslaught*. Moreover, they remember well his relentless efforts and focus to "reform the judiciary" against the will of the people, which would have severely undercut Israel's democracy, while he is also facing three criminal charges against him, all while Hamas was readying itself for its unfathomable savagery of innocent Israelis. Regardless of how the Israel-Hamas war ends and how politically savvy and manipulative Netanyahu may be, there is an overwhelming public consensus that he will be ousted even if the elections are held in six months or more. A new centrist and left-of-center government, potentially led by Benny Gantz, the leader of the National Unity party, will be open to negotiating in good faith the establishment of a Palestinian state.

Given the unending violent conflict culminating with Hamas' attack, the *continued occupation is unsustainable and will diminish Israel as we know it*. Before October 7th, this view was on display from such high-profile Israelis as Tamir Pardo, former Mossad chief, who stated that the occupation is an "existential threat" to the country.[lx] Even after the attack, opposition leaders such as Labour MK Gilad Kariv have outlined the threat, stating that "Right now, the extreme settlers are violating Israeli law, and they are harming the ability of Israel to meet or to face its real enemies, meaning Hamas and Hezbollah."[lxi]

Furthermore, there is growing public sentiment among Israelis that the occupation is a threat to Israel; despite the turmoil, 56 percent of Israelis reject the idea of reoccupying Gaza and reestablishing settlements.[lxii] Israel will become a pariah state if it isn't already—a garrison country, an occupier that lives by the gun, defying international laws and consensus, alienating its best friends, betraying its founders' vision, and shattering the Jews' two-millennia-long dream of a Jewish state that is free, secure, proud, and at peace.

Reform of the Palestinian Authority

Although the Palestinian Authority has recognized Israel, it must now seize the unsurpassed opportunity to realize its aspiration for statehood. Given, however, the utter lack of popularity of the Palestinian Authority under Abbas and endemic corruption, the Palestinians must also prepare for free new elections. Abbas may be offered a ceremonial position, but he *must step aside.* The newly emerging political parties in the West Bank and Gaza *should be allowed to participate in the election regardless of their political and ideological leaning.* As a sign of good faith, Israel should agree to release Marwan Barghouti, who is a moderate, is held in high esteem, and believes in a two-state solution. As director of the Palestinian Center for Policy and Survey Research, Khalil Shikaki stated, "Barghouti is the single most popular leader alive."[lxiii] Other prominent Palestinian leaders should also be released from prison in order to participate in elections, provided that they renounce violence.

Certainly, we cannot rule out the emergence of new Palestinian parties in a new election that may not support a two-state solution. But, based on the current Palestinian Authority's stance, any emerging parties will have the knowledge that they will not be able to form a government that stands against a two-state solution if it wants a chance at peace with Israel. They must choose between proceeding with a two-state solution or having no state at all. I feel strongly that they will opt for the former option.

There are many Palestinians and some Israelis who prefer a democratic one-state solution, especially given the interspersed Israeli and Palestinian populations in the West Bank, Jerusalem, Israel proper, and the proximity of the Palestinians in Gaza, which is a non-starter for the vast majority of Israelis. Some Israelis prefer the current "one-state reality," which is tantamount to an apartheid state and is categorically unacceptable to the Palestinians.

Based on what we know already, the Arab states are extremely frustrated with the Palestinian position and have threatened the Palestinian Authority that they will proceed with normalization of relations with Israel as the UAE, Bahrain, and Morocco have done. In practical terms, they put the PA on notice that unless they show flexibility and negotiate in good faith toward a two-state solution, the Palestinians will be left to their own devices and will no longer be able to rely on the Arab states for political or even financial support.

WHY THE TWO-STATE SOLUTION IS THE ONLY VIABLE OPTION TO THE EXCLUSION OF ANY OTHER[23]

Although the two-state solution has been the only viable option that best serves Israel's national security and political interests and meets the Palestinians' national aspiration for statehood, the Israel-Hamas war has only reaffirmed that there is no other option.

The Israel-Hamas war has reignited discussions over a two-state solution as an end to the Israeli-Palestinian conflict. Those who closely monitor the conflict and consider its history, the psychological mindset of both peoples, and their affinity and mutual claims to the same land, cannot escape the conclusion that a two-state solution is the only practical and sustainable option. Other "options" have circulated, but careful examination shows that none are viable—nor is the status quo, which is unsustainable, as demonstrated by the Israel-Hamas war and the unprecedented spike in violence in the West Bank.

After 57 years of occupation, Israeli-Palestinian relations are worse than ever before. Indeed, we have never seen this level of violence that has robbed the lives of so many Israelis and Palestinians and rained havoc and destruction. This attests to the dismal failure of both sides to accept that *neither has an exclusive right to the entire land* stretching from the Mediterranean to the Jordan River and that only two independent states would usher in a permanent solution to their endemic conflict.

Sadly, it took the Israel-Hamas war to awaken both sides to their tragic reality. They must now realize there will be no return to the status quo ante. The circumstances that led to the Israel-Hamas war only reinforced the inescapable requirement for a two-state solu-

23 A version of this chapter was originally published in CNN Arabic (Alon Ben-Meir, "رأي.. لماذا يعتبر حل الدولتين الخيار الوحيد القابل للتطبيق؟," CNN, December 26, 2023, https://arabic.cnn.com/middle-east/article/2023/12/26/two-states-solution-oped-alon-ben-meir.)

tion. Simply put, there is no other viable option other than continuing the bloody conflict for decades to come.

Option One: Maintaining the Status Quo

This war, instigated by Hamas' unprecedented slaughter of 1,200 Israelis, has inflicted horrifying destruction in Gaza and resulted in the death of more than 30,000 Palestinians at the time of writing, 70 percent of whom are women and children.[lxiv] This tragic development has demonstrated the colossal failure of successive Netanyahu-led Israeli governments, which believed they could indefinitely maintain the occupation of the West Bank and the blockade of Gaza to prevent the Palestinians from establishing a state of their own.

The nearly six decades of occupation, which were punctuated by violence, Intifadas, terrorism, and mini-wars, have not seemed to faze Netanyahu and his hard-core followers. They maintain that the casualties that Israel has sustained over these years were a price worth paying for what they deemed "protecting Israel"—translating to keeping the occupation in place and expanding the settlements. Meanwhile, some ministers have been implicitly encouraging the settlers to harass Palestinians in the West Bank, engaging in systematic dehumanization and creating unbearable conditions for Palestinians, forcing many of them to abandon their land.

The preservation of the status quo has created a *de facto one state*, which successive Israeli governments sought all along by applying one set of civilian laws for the Israeli Jews who live in the West Bank and martial law for the Palestinians, which amounted to nothing less than apartheid.

During the past 16 years in power, Netanyahu deliberately portrayed the Palestinians as an irredeemable mortal foe that must be fought with an iron fist, and justified the continuing occupation as a means by which to quell Palestinian resistance and prevent them from ever establishing their own state. In December 2023,

Netanyahu stated: "I'm proud that I prevented the establishment of a Palestinian state because today everybody understands what the Palestinian state could have been, now that we've seen the little Palestinian state in Gaza. Everyone understands what would have happened if we had capitulated to international pressures and enabled a state like that in Judaea and Samaria [the West Bank]."[lxv]

By making such a statement, Netanyahu put his hypocrisy on full display. No Israeli leader has helped strengthen Hamas more than Netanyahu, as he allowed billions of dollars from Qatar to flow into its coffers. For him, the Palestinian Authority is a liability and Hamas is an asset—a sentiment that he articulated time and again. Furthermore, Israel's withdrawal from Gaza in 2005 was precipitous, with no security arrangements made with the PA. The Sharon government fully knew at the time that Hamas was by far superior militarily to the PA and would take over Gaza. But Netanyahu's distortion of the truth is what defines him, as no one wanted to split Hamas and the PA to prevent the establishment of a Palestinian state more than him.

The Israel-Hamas war has glaringly demonstrated that the occupation is not sustainable, the blockade of Gaza is logistically unsustainable as it allowed Hamas to build a formidable offensive military capacity under the watchful eyes of Israel, and Hamas' designs to liquidate Israel have proven to be nothing but nightmarish illusions to the detriment of the Palestinian people.

Option Two: The One-state Option

The Palestinians would accept a democratic one-state solution if all citizens, Israeli Jews and Palestinians alike, enjoy equal rights before the law, participate in free and fair elections, run for office, and the winner in general elections forms a government representative of the peoples' votes. This kind of one-state solution, though it sounds fair and democratic, *is categorically unacceptable to the Israelis* because of demographic realities. There are nearly 3 million Palestinians in the West Bank, 2.1 million in Gaza, and about

2 million in Israel proper, which combined is more than 7 million, approximately equal to the Jewish population in Israel.[24]

The Palestinians would welcome such a solution because, in a free and fair election, they could win a majority vote and potentially form a Palestinian-dominated government in Israel, if not now, certainly within three to five years. Such a prospect would *defy the very reason behind Israel's creation* as a Jewish state that offers a home to any Jew who chooses to live in the country, which *no Israeli government will ever accept.*

Option Three: Autonomous Palestinian Entity

The failure to advance a two-state solution in the past prompted some academics and Arab officials weary of the persistent conflict to think of a different option, a compromise whereby the Palestinians in the West Bank and Gaza could establish *their own entity* that would enjoy autonomous rule. This would encompass all of Areas A and B, 80-90 percent of Area C, and all of Gaza.[25] Besides having internal security, this entity would be demilitarized but maintain overall security in full cooperation with Israel. This solution would technically end the occupation.

This option has not gained much traction because the Palestinians insist that they have an inalienable right to establish *an independent Palestinian state in the West Bank and Gaza,* with its capital in Jerusalem. Conversely, Israel has insisted all along that it will not relinquish overall security control, as that would risk its own security. Neither Israel nor the Palestinians have seriously considered this option mainly because, for Israel, it leaves the settlements in a pre-

---

24 All demographic statistics are from *The World Factbook.*

25 Currently, Area A, approximately 18 percent of the West Bank's total territory, is fully administered by the Palestinian Authority. In Area B (22 percent), the PA controls civilian affairs while sharing security control with Israel. Area C represents 60 percent of the West Bank's land mass and is fully under Israeli control. See https://www.anera.org/what-are-area-a-area-b-and-area-c-in-the-west-bank/.

carious state in terms of its security, governance, and development, and for the Palestinians, it is not full-fledged sovereignty.

And there is the *inconceivably sick option* wherein extremists on both sides—messianic Israeli Jews and Palestinian jihadis—seek to expel or even liquidate the other from any territory they currently occupy, which deserves no elaboration but only the strongest condemnation for even thinking in those terms which is akin to ethnic cleansing and absolute sheer madness.

None of the above options had any chance of materializing, which brings us to the fourth and only viable option.

Option Four: The Two-state Solution

The two-state solution—independent states that exist side-by-side, respect each other's sovereignty and rights, and live in peace and security—is *the only viable option*. Given the dramatically changing conditions on the ground since 1967, a high level of collaboration between them becomes *sine qua non* and supportive of a sustainable two-state solution.

First, Israelis and Palestinians are interspersed in the West Bank, Jerusalem, and Israel proper. There are an estimated 3.1 million Palestinians and 700,000 Israelis in the West Bank and East Jerusalem, and roughly 1.9 million Israeli Arab citizens.[lxvi] Since it is simply impossible to relocate a large segment of either population either voluntarily or by force, or change their demographic makeup, it makes *the coexistence of Israelis and Palestinians inescapable*.

Second, Israel's national security and the Palestinians' sense of insecurity are sources of great concern to both sides. Therefore, security collaboration is central to any peace agreement. Even now, there is *extensive security cooperation between the PA and Israel*. Any peace agreement should expand upon the existing security arrangement between them. Moreover, the Palestinian state must be demilitarized and join the ranks of over 20 countries that do not have a standing military force, including Iceland, Panama, Haiti,

Mauritius, and Monaco.[lxvii] This would *categorically refute* the claim by many Israelis, including Netanyahu, that a newly established Palestinian state in the West Bank would pose an existential threat to Israel.

Third, solutions to the main conflicting issues, including Jerusalem, the settlements and the Palestinian refugees, can be found only within the two states framework. In principle, given the religious and historical affinity of Israelis and Palestinians to Jerusalem, it will remain united as neither side wants to redivide the city. The three blocks of settlements along the 1967 borders which house 80 percent of the settlers will remain in place, and many smaller settlements will be relocated to allow for a contiguous Palestinian state. The solution to the Palestinian refugees will be based on re-settlement and/or compensation. Negotiations along these lines between Israel and the Palestinians have taken place in the past and have nearly reached agreements on all three issues. Further details on those conflicting issues are in my proposal for an Israeli-Palestinian-Jordanian confederation, published in *World Affairs*.[26]

Counter Arguments to a Two-State Solution

There are generally four categories of arguments against the two-state solution as the only viable option. The first is that this is not the right time, given the Israel-Hamas war, and it will take another generation before Israelis and Palestinians can reconcile and begin peace talks. The second argument is that the Palestinians will never accept Israel's right to exist even if they established a state of their own, as they are bent on Israel's destruction. The third category believes the whole idea of a two-state solution is akin to satire and does not warrant serious consideration. The fourth argument is that the conflict is endemic and irreconcilable, and thus, the whole notion of a two-state solution is illusionary and will never happen.

What is troubling about these views is the resignation that any re-

---

26 See Alon Ben-Meir, "The Case for an Israeli-Palestinian-Jordanian Confederation."

newed peace negotiation will be futile because everything that has been tried before to reach a peace agreement did not work. I vehemently disagree because this conflict, which has already inflicted so much death and destruction on both sides over the past 76 years, *will never go away* and will continue to haunt them for generations until they face their current disastrous reality.

"This Is Not the Right Time"

For those who claim this is not the right time, I ask, when is the right time? Do the Israelis and Palestinians need more time to inflict hundreds of thousands more casualties before waking up to their tragic existence? More time to poison another four generations with enmity and venom toward the other? More time to dehumanize the other, to make the killing and savagery of innocent people casual? More time to squander billions for training, procuring military hardware, and preparing the young to die in the next war? More time to conspire and collude to terrorize the other? More time for millions to suffer, feel threatened, and live in fear and agonizing uncertainty? More time to deepen the hatred, animosity, and distrust to make reconciliation impossible? And more time to shatter the dream of the vast majority on both sides to live in peace and security?

Now *is* the time to end the conflict because *more time will make it even more intractable* and exact an ever-higher price in blood and precious resources, and as the conflict continues, they will still face one another in war or in peace because their coexistence in one form or another is inescapable.

"The Palestinians Are Bent on Israel's Destruction"

There are indeed many extremist Palestinians, such as Hamas and Islamic Jihad, who are committed to Israel's destruction and will not abandon their plan to destroy Israel even if the Palestinians establish a state of their own. But then, 76 years later, they have nothing to show for it. There is no Palestinian state and they are subjected to occupation under which they are losing ground every passing day. They never had the means to pose a clear and present danger to Israel and will never acquire a military edge over Israel. The Israel-Hamas war is only demonstrating Hamas' calamitous miscalculation, as their savagery of innocent Israelis will end up eviscerating the movement to the point of no return.

Surely, there will still be fanatics who revel in self-deception, believing they can still destroy Israel, but here is where it will end in self-deceit. The Palestinian Authority, a multitude of Palestinian moderates, and the leading Arab states have long since accepted Israel's existence. This goes back to the Arab Peace Initiative in 2002, representing a major transformation from the Arab League's Khartoum Resolution of September 1967, known for its three Nos—no negotiation, no recognition, and no peace. The Abraham Accords further attest to the Arab states' attitude toward Israel, which has not been lost on the Palestinians. Even Hamas' own charter, updated in 2017, accepts a Palestinian state based on the 1967 borders—a recognition, albeit implicit, that Israel does and will continue to exist.[lxviii]

"The Idea of a Two-state Solution is Akin to Satire"

Some opponents to the two-state solution refer to the idea as satire and intimate that only the naïve would still advocate for such a foolish proposal. Well, I do not find the continuing death of Israelis and Palestinians by the thousands funny, nor do I view the indiscriminate killing of Israeli men, women, and children by Palestinian terrorists as amusing. I do not think that the occupation and the frequent Palestinian casualties in the West Bank are a laughing matter, nor do I find the horrifying savagery and mutilation of women by Hamas hysterical. I do not believe wars that cause so much havoc, destruction, tragic loss of life, and starvation of children are humorous, nor do I see the continuing suppression of Palestinians under occupation as comical. I do not find the indoctrination of Palestinian youth to hate and violently resist the Israelis hilarious, nor do I find the Israelis' view that the Palestinians are a perpetual mortal enemy entertaining.

This madness must stop, and nothing will stop it unless Israel and the Palestinians agree on a two-state solution. However doubtful many on both sides are about such an end-game, no one has come up as yet with a realistic alternative to end four generations of bloody conflict.

"A Two-state Solution Is an Illusion"

Finally, there are those who claim that the two-state solution is nothing but an illusion that will never come to pass simply because neither Israel nor the Palestinians will ever agree to share the land from the Mediterranean to the Jordan River, which each considers to be exclusively theirs. To make their case, they submit that for the past seven decades, nothing has worked—incentives, compromises, pressure, persuasion, peace negotiations, the threat of violence, mediation, international conferences or UN resolutions, summits, or interim agreements—and there is nothing left that can facilitate a solution. For all they know, it is illusionary to think that the conflict could end with a two-state solution because it is endemic and has become an intrinsic module of Israeli and Palestinian DNA.

I disagree with this argument, which assumes that there are conflicts that cannot be resolved. There are ample examples of violent conflicts that ended peacefully. Whereas past efforts to resolve the Israeli-Palestinian conflict have failed, *sometimes it takes a major explosion* to shake the dynamic of the conflict fundamentally. Hamas' unprecedented gruesome attack and Israel's unparalleled retaliation have done exactly that. They dramatically upended the dynamic of the conflict and created new conditions between the two sides, making it impossible for them to simply return to the status quo ante, which has never been sustainable.

The ultimate defeat of Hamas as a political force offers a historic opportunity to end the Israeli-Palestinian conflict that must not be missed. Unlike any other time in the past, the two-state solution is now back at the front and center of any future Israeli and Palestinian discourse and is seen as the only viable option. It will take, though, new, courageous, and visionary leaders on both sides to seize this generational opportunity.

Of course, it will take some time for both sides to act, but the time of reckoning has arrived.

THE FOUR KEY PLAYERS

Saudi Arabia's Position

Saudi Arabia has been negotiating normalization of relations with Israel behind the scenes, and in spite of the Israel-Hamas war, Riyadh reiterated its willingness to do so, *provided that Israel agrees to the establishment of an independent Palestinian state* and that the US meets three conditions: guaranteeing Saudi Arabia's national security through a defense treaty, allowing Riyadh to acquire a nascent nuclear program for peaceful purposes, and facilitating the purchase of advanced military hardware. The Saudis have privately intimated that the speed and the scope of the normalization process with Israel will have to correspond to the progress made in the Israeli-Palestinian peace talks, which would help keep the negotiations on track, provide incentives, and maintain momentum while encouraging other Arab states to follow suit in the spirit of the Arab Peace Initiative.

Saudi Arabia's role in advancing an Israeli-Palestinian peace agreement is more critical at this juncture than at any time before. Saudi Arabia has no conflict with Israel; in fact, it has extended conditional recognition of Israel as far back as 2002 when it introduced the Arab Peace Initiative (API). The API offered Israel normalization of relations with the Arab states in exchange for returning Palestinian land captured by Israel in the Six Day War of 1967 and settling the conflict with the Palestinians based on a two-state solution. As recently as 2018, Saudi Arabia's Crown Prince Mohammed bin Salman stated, "I believe the Palestinians and the Israelis have the right to have their own land. But we have to have a peace agreement to assure the stability for everyone and to have normal relations."[lxix]

Saudi Arabia's role in any future Israeli-Palestinian will be central for several reasons. Saudi Arabia is the birthplace of Islam and the site of its holiest shrines; it is fitting that Crown Prince Mohammed bin Salman noted, "We have religious concerns about the fate of the holy mosque in Jerusalem and about the rights of the Palestinian people … we don't have any objection against any other people."[lxx] Indeed, as the global leader of Sunni Islam, Saudi Arabia has intrinsic concerns over the future of Jerusalem, which is the home of the Sunni Muslims' third holiest shrines at Haram al-Sharif—the al-Aqsa Mosque and the Dome of Rock. In this regard, the Saudis feel strongly that East Jerusalem should be the capital of the Palestinians' future state. This position was the central issue that proved to be a sticking point, and it remains so in continuing back-channel dialogue between Saudis and Israelis.

Given the changing political and security dynamic in the region and the frustration with the never-ending Palestinian cause, the Saudis strongly feel that ending the Israeli-Palestinian conflict will alleviate some of the more pressing regional tensions. To that end, they have tacitly supported the UAE, Bahrain, Sudan, and Morocco in normalizing relations with Israel. By deciding to make their existing cooperation and relationship with Israel an open secret, they are indirectly increasing the pressure on the Palestinians to demonstrate more flexibility lest they be left alone to fend for themselves, which thus far has only undermined rather than enhanced their cause.

Ending the Israeli-Palestinian conflict would allow the Saudis to normalize relations with Israel, which will have many significant and positive regional implications from which Saudi Arabia can greatly benefit. From a national security perspective, the Saudis see eye-to-eye with Israel concerning Iran, as they view its growing influence in the region as a threat to their national security. The Saudis acknowledge the Jewish state as the region's foremost military power, capable of halting Iran's hegemonic ambition—for example, by consistently attacking Iranian military installations in Syria to prevent Tehran from establishing a permanent foothold in the country, disrupting Iran's nuclear weapon program, and intercepting shipments of weapons to radical groups such as Hezbollah, Hamas, and Islamic Jihad, which reduces Iran's ability to destabilize the region.

In addition, the Saudis are also very interested in Israel's advanced technology. They can benefit from its impressive innovations in many fields, including medicine, agriculture, water security, cybersecurity, energy, desalination technology, and industrial developments. In fact, for the past several years, Israel and Saudi Arabia have been cooperating on a number of fronts, including in the transfer of Israeli technology, strategic coordination, and intelligence-sharing, the latter of which goes back more than two decades.[lxxi] And to further demonstrate their growing cooperation with Israel, following the Abraham Accords, the Saudis are now allowing Israeli flights to use its air space for the first time.

Israel, on the other hand, strongly wants to normalize relations with Saudi Arabia because of its unique position and power in the Arab world and its ability to set trends for the Arab and broader Muslim world. As such, for Israel, normalization with Saudi Arabia would also prompt normalization of relations with many other predominantly Muslim states far beyond the four of the Abraham Accords. In so doing, they open the door for Israel to discover the wide-ranging benefits normalization would bring, including trade, extensive security collaboration, and a host of other benefits, including joint development projects. However, as long as the Israeli-Palestinian conflict remains unresolved, diplomatic relations between Israel and Saudi Arabia will have to wait. For this reason, as long as Saudi Arabia withholds its recognition, the pressure on Israel to resolve the conflict with the Palestinians will continue to mount.

Conversely, given Saudi Arabia's unique status, Riyadh can exert tremendous influence over the Palestinian Authority. The Saudis have been extremely disappointed with the PA, especially with President Abbas and his lieutenants, whom they accuse of being corrupt, disloyal, and ungrateful for all the help that has been extended to them. Having been consistent, however, in their support of a Palestinian state, they can exert tremendous pressure on the PA, especially because Palestinian leaders badly need Saudi Arabia's political and financial support. As one case in point, given the fact that resettling and/or compensating the Palestinian refugees is central to ending the Israeli-Palestinian conflict, Saudi Arabia has the sway and the ability, above other Arab states, to contribute and raise billions of dollars from other Arab oil-producing countries to that end.

The fact that the Palestinian problem is also a subject of public discussions which Riyadh cannot ignore makes it much harder for the Saudi government to make public their growing closeness to Israel, let alone fully normalize relations. As such, they made it clear to the Israelis that unless Israel reaches a peace agreement with the Palestinians based on a two-state solution, Saudi Arabia will not normalize relations with the Jewish state as they see that as *a betrayal of their more than two-decades-long advocacy.*

Finally, due to the fact that from their own vantage point, both Israel and the Palestinians need Saudi Arabia, the Saudis can help facilitate the negotiating process and also monitor the Israeli-Palestinian talks to ensure that both sides negotiate in good faith. Indeed, in the context of confederation, which the Saudis may well strongly endorse because it meets their requirements, neither Israel nor the Palestinians can ignore the Saudi position, whose support they need under any circumstances.

Jordan's Position[27]

For many reasons—including Jordan's national security concerns, its proximity to Israel and the West Bank, the demographic composition of the country (wherein approximately 55 percent of Jordanians are of Palestinian descent),[lxxii] commercial ties with both Israel and the Palestinians, Jordan's custodianship of the Muslim holy shrines in Jerusalem, and being at peace with Israel, and regardless of the eventual contours of the Israeli-Palestinian peace—Jordan is a central player in the Israeli-Palestinian conflict and needs to play

---

27   From Alon Ben-Meir, "The Case for an Israeli-Palestinian-Jordanian Confederation: Why Now and How?"

a pivotal role in facilitating the Israeli-Palestinian negotiations due to its national interest, which is intertwined with both Israel and the Palestinians. Jordan shares a nearly 350 km border with Israel and the West Bank. This shared border has serious implications for almost every aspect of life between them. Thus, Jordan's input from the onset of the negotiations is crucial for the sustainability of a future Israel-Palestinian peace agreement.

The Israeli-Jordanian Peace

Since the peace treaty between Israel and Jordan was signed in 1994, the late King Hussein and his successor, King Abdullah, carefully guarded the peace treaty by maintaining mutually beneficial relations between the two countries. Occasionally, they experienced some tension, mostly connected to Israel's treatment of Palestinians in the territories, the building of settlements in the West Bank, and security and access disputes over the Temple Mount. Apart from these issues, regardless of who led the Israeli government and their political leanings, Jordan made it a point to focus on its national interests first.

Although Jordan denounces the occupation, objects to Israel's building and expanding settlements in the West Bank, and condemns Israel's harsh treatment of the Palestinians and the annexation of Palestinian territories, among other disputes, Amman has not allowed such disagreements to affect the fundamentals of the peace treaty with Israel. Jordan views its peace with Israel as one of the most important pillars of the country's geostrategic interests and political stability. On the other hand, although Israel often complained about Jordan's unwillingness to reveal any of the benefits it has derived from the peace treaty due to not wanting to compromise its public unwavering support of the Palestinians, Israel did not allow this "cold peace" to compromise the integrity or affect the strategic importance of the peace treaty with Jordan. That said, the Jordanians are increasingly concerned about the ultimate intention of the current extremist right-wing Israeli government and its endgame regarding the Israeli-Palestinian conflict and how that might affect Jordan.

Indeed, from the Jordanian perspective, peace with Israel has offered the Hashemite Kingdom many advantages that outweigh any discord between the two countries. Although much of the collaboration between Jordan and Israel on many fronts receives little publicity, it is extensive and continues to grow. One other element that keeps the bilateral relations on track is that Israel uses its influence on its congressional supporters in Washington to ensure continuing financial aid to Jordan to the tune of $1.5 billion, which further cements the Israeli-Jordanian bilateral relationship.[lxxiii] The fact that the US views both Israel and Jordan as strategic allies further deepens their ties, which has significant regional implications.

Intertwined National Security

Perhaps the most noteworthy aspect of Israeli-Jordanian relations is their comprehensive security collaboration which, in fact, served as the bedrock that has sustained and further strengthened their peace treaty. This security collaboration entails military-to-military relations, including intelligence sharing, military training, the transfer of military technology, and the purchase of light weapons from Israel. This is particularly important because the threats emanating from Iran and its militant proxies in Syria, Lebanon, and Iraq affect both countries' national security. For Israel, ensuring stability in Jordan is vital to its national security, and from the Jordanian perspective, Israel provides significant deterrence against any enemy that seeks to undermine the Kingdom's security.

In addition, Jordan provides Israel with strategic depth to the east, which is in concert with the US defense strategy in the Middle East. The US in particular considers the peace treaty to be extremely important for American strategic interests, and it has prioritized improving ties between the two countries. To be sure, both benefit greatly from their security cooperation, which continues to expand due to the unsettling regional conflicts. Finally, the current Israeli-Jordanian security cooperation will continue to provide a solid foundation for the creation of a united security apparatus that includes the Palestinians. Indeed, Israel's present security collaboration with both Jordan and the Palestinian Authority is intertwined and trilaterally complementary.

Custodianship of the Muslim Holy Shrines

Since the signing of the peace treaty between Israel and Jordan, Israel has always respected the Hashemite Kingdom's special role in administering the Muslim and Christian holy sites in Jerusalem,[28] which gives Jordan significant input over the status quo on the Temple Mount. Amman has often been at odds with Israel for not enforcing the ban on Israeli Jews praying at the al-Aqsa compound, which is a violation of the status quo. Amman also criticizes Israel for its heavy-handed security around the compound and access to it, most recently seen in the aftermath of Israeli restrictions on access to the holy site during Ramadan in April 2021. Nevertheless, the two sides quickly reconciled, as neither wanted any conflict to impact their relationship adversely.

It is important to note that since Jordan's custodianship of the Muslim holy shrines is not likely to change, it will not have a dramatic impact on the final solution to Jerusalem. Jordan is committed to the establishment of a Palestinian state, and it respects Israel's sovereign right to control, administer, and further develop its own holy sites. It does not, however, view that as an obstacle in the search for a solution to East Jerusalem, which is mutually claimed by Israel and the Palestinians.

Jordan's Demographic Composition

King Abdullah is sensitive to the large number of people of Palestinian descent in his country, which comprise more than 50 percent of the Jordanian population.[29] The vast majority of Pales-

---

28 With the exception of Roman Catholic sites.

29 This number is disputed; a Jordanian official claimed in a conversation with

tinians who were born in Jordan view themselves as full-fledged Jordanian citizens, yet still have a very deep affinity to all Palestinians, regardless of their places of residence, and strongly support the establishment of an independent Palestinian state in the West Bank and Gaza.

Jordan lost its control over the West Bank following the 1967 Six Day War and, by 1988, fully relinquished its claim, because the late King Hussein wanted to separate the West Bank from Jordan proper. He sought, and his successor King Abdullah continued, not only to safeguard Jordan's territorial integrity and political independence but also to *disabuse many Israelis of the notion that Jordan is Palestinian*, as the premise that the Palestinians had a homeland in Jordan fueled justifications for annexing the West Bank. Jordan has and continues to insist, particularly since 1988, that the Palestinians in the West Bank and Gaza have an inalienable right to establish a state of their own with East Jerusalem as its capital. Both kings steadfastly opposed the occupation and the expansion of the settlements, and certainly any further annexation of Palestinian land.

In fact, Jordan made it very clear that if Israel is to annex a large part of the West Bank, Amman may well sever its diplomatic relations with Israel. King Abdullah's position has undoubtedly greatly inhibited Israel from taking such a step, especially in the wake of the Abraham Accords with the United Arab Emirates, Bahrain, Sudan, and Morocco. The four countries have likewise insisted that their normalization of relations with Israel is conditioned upon Israel's ceasing any further annexation of Palestinian land in the West Bank.

For Jordan, the establishment of a Palestinian state would lay to rest the Palestinian refugee problem, which has, over the years, been threatening Jordan's stability and the region as a whole. Thus, under conditions of Israeli-Palestinian peace, the Palestinian refugees who want to settle in the West Bank and Gaza and those who

---

the author that the real number of Jordanians of Palestinian descent is between 43 and 48 percent.

seek compensation and remain in their places of residence will be able to do so—which is the only practical outcome under any circumstances.

Jordan's Commercial Ties

Any analysis of the economic and commercial ties between Israel, Jordan, and the PA suggests that all stand to considerably gain in these areas beyond what they have achieved thus far. Despite the occasional political squabbles between Jordan and Israel, and tension and punctuated violence between Israel and the Palestinians, their economic and commercial ties are steadily increasing and greatly contributing to the durability of their relationship. The immediate fruit of the Israel-Jordanian peace was financial; due to the 1994 treaty, the US began foreign debt relief and restructuring arrangements totaling over $3 billion.[lxxiv] In the years since, Jordan and Israel have signed deals for natural gas and water, and Israel has allowed a significant increase in Jordanian exports to Palestinians in the West Bank. In addition, they agreed on a gradual reduction of customs tariffs, and duties were abolished on many products traded between them. Besides direct trade, Jordan serves as a bridge for Israel to the large market of the Gulf states and other large Arab countries. In addition, two trade deals signed between the two with Western powers—one with the US, another with the EU—allowed Jordan to benefit from Israel's preexisting agreements with both powers.

The environment has been another beneficiary of increased Jordanian-Israeli-Palestinian cooperation. A landmark agreement signed between the three parties and the World Bank in 2013 supported the management of limited water resources and the usage of desalinated water, which Israel is a leader in producing. In addition, all three governments agreed to collaborate on cleaning the Jordan River in 2015, knowing that only through cooperation can they serve their own interest, which has become increasingly clear over the past decades.[lxxv]

Jordan is in need of investments in infrastructure, Israel wants to expand its regional legitimacy, and the Palestinians want political recognition. These kinds of projects and cooperation strongly suggest that the three countries can and indeed must work together and offer a joint, wide-ranging plan for a high level of cooperation. The above strongly suggests that Jordan will have to play a significant role in the search for an Israeli-Palestinian peace agreement and why its full cooperation to realize that goal is indispensable.

Egypt's Position

When Egypt and Israel signed a peace agreement in 1979, the two countries developed a good working relationship, which continued to improve and expand over the years, albeit with little public exposure, especially because of the continuing Israeli-Palestinian conflict and the Egyptian public's support of the Palestinian cause. Egypt was the first Arab country to realize that Israel is a significant military power that it cannot defeat. Then-President Anwar Sadat decided that his country would benefit greatly from peace with Israel rather than maintaining a state of hostility. Sadat invited the Palestinians to join the peace negotiations with Israel but was rebuffed, and ever since, the Palestinians' conflict with Israel has become ever more intractable with occasional periods of calm but without any progress on the peace front.

Egypt has had and continues to have national security concerns regarding Gaza. Since President Sisi came to power in 2013, the security cooperation between Israel and Egypt has accelerated, reaching an extraordinary level unseen before. Both countries share many common objectives, especially countering Islamic radicalism, containing Iran's regional influence, maintaining peace in the Sinai Peninsula, and countering Palestinian extremism in Gaza. Egypt views an Israeli-Palestinian peace as pivotal to its own and the region's stability and has often played an important role in mitigating conflicting issues between Israel and the Palestinians.

Egypt's relationship with Hamas was and still is adversarial at best, as Cairo views Hamas as an offshoot of the Muslim Brotherhood, which Sisi labeled a terrorist organization in 2013.[lxxvi] Two years later, Egypt classified Hamas—both its political and military wings—as a terrorist organization as well (albeit the designation was overturned by an Egyptian court months later) and restricted its movement from and to Gaza through the Rafah crossing, which is one of only two crossings for the Palestinians in Gaza to the outside world.[lxxvii]

Regardless of how the Israel-Hamas war ends and what kind of governing authority will be in place, Egypt remains a significant player in any future peace negotiations between Israel and the Palestinians. In the past, Egyptian security officials helped on multiple occasions to mediate between Israel and Hamas in order to defuse tension between the two sides, especially following three prior wars between Israel and Hamas. Since the October 2023 Israel-Hamas war broke out, Egypt has and will continue to play a central role in the search for Israeli-Palestinian peace.

In a July 2021 meeting between Egypt Foreign Minister Sameh Shoukry and his then-Israeli counterpart Yair Lapid, Shoukry emphasized "the need to resolve the current stalemate between the Palestinian and Israeli sides, leading to just and comprehensive peace negotiations."[lxxviii] Indeed, Egypt sees itself as the guardian of the Palestinian cause because of its importance to the Egyptian public and the government itself, which wants to be viewed as a central player in mitigating the Israeli-Palestinian conflict or engaging in any future peace process.

Egypt's importance in helping forge an Israeli-Palestinian peace agreement cannot be overstated. But for Egypt to play such an important role, it must translate its influence into action. In this regard, it should make it abundantly clear to the Palestinians that if they want to establish a state of their own, grow, survive, and flourish, their only option is to negotiate with Israel in good faith and renounce violence in all forms. Egypt's message to Israel is that there is no other option to ending the Israeli-Palestinian conflict unless it is based on a two-state solution.

As far as Egypt's role in dealing with Hamas in the future, that is obviously going to depend on how the war is going to end, whether or not Hamas is crushed politically, and if any elements of Hamas will remain, which is more than likely. The question then will be whether or not Hamas wants to join the peace process or remain as a resistance movement. In this regard, Israel and Egypt ought to be on the same page in addressing this still open-ended issue. One thing, however, should be clear. Once Israel withdraws from Gaza and the Palestinian Authority transitions into power, the blockade must gradually come to an end, obviously, with all the security apparatus to be established to prevent the reoccurrence of what happened when Israel withdrew from Gaza precipitously in 2005, without making ironclad security arrangements with the then-Palestinian Authority that was in charge of Gaza.

The US Position

Successive American administrations have advocated for a two-state solution. They paid, however, no more than lip service to the idea. In the wake of the Israel-Hamas war, President Biden, more than any of his predecessors, has repeatedly raised the issue and insisted in conversations with Netanyahu that it's time for Israel to come around and face the inevitable. *A two-state solution is the only viable option* that will solve the Israeli-Palestinian conflict and end decades of death and destruction, stabilize the region, strengthen Israel's national security, and usher in a new era of regional peace and prosperity.

Unlike other relationships with allies, the Israel-US relationship is unique on many different levels, and it has been as such from the time Israel was established in 1948. The uniqueness of their relationship is anchored on three pillars that have remained consistent throughout the years because, in some way, Israel's security, well-being, and future as an independent democratic state with shared values has become almost a domestic issue in the US that has enjoyed bipartisan support, which has not significantly vacillated over the years, irrespective of the changing geopolitical conditions in the Middle East.

1. **Moral commitment:** The US moral commitment emanated from the experience of the European Jews during World War II that culminated in the Holocaust, which claimed the lives of six million Jews. The creation of the State of Israel from the ashes of that unparalleled genocide has become ingrained in the conscience of the majority of the American people.

2. **Political support:** Israel has enjoyed political support from many streams of the US political landscape. The United States, under both Democratic and Republican administrations, sees Israel as an extension of the American experiment. Although the US moral commitment has a direct effect on its political backing, it is also affected by the unequivocal support of Evangelical Christians to Israel's security and continued existence, as Israel is viewed as indispensable to the return of the Messiah. Given the massive political sway and importance of the Evangelical vote, Republicans have sought their political support in any national and local elections. Moreover, as a broad swath of Americans—Republicans (including Evangelicals), independents, and moderate Democrats included, all of whom Democrats need to court electorally—support Israel, Democratic politicians remain staunch in their support for the country as well.[lxxix]

3. **Strategic interest:** Given the US strategic interest in the Middle East, Israel had become a significant asset as both countries found a common interest in collaborating on a range of significant issues, including intelligence sharing, the development of advanced technology, the testing of new military hardware, and training, among many others. The US commitment to Israel's national security became ironclad, and regardless of the occasional disagreement on certain issues, that commitment remains solid.

There are three glaring examples of the allies' major disagreements.

The first is over the settlements enterprise, to which successive American administrations objected firmly and to which Israel has continued to defy the American position with impunity. The second is the divergence in their assessment of Iran's nuclear program and what to do about it. And the third is over the Netanyahu government's efforts to reform the judiciary, which could have severely undermined Israel's democracy and which runs contrary to American values. However, these differences, among others, still have not shaken the strong foundation of US-Israel bilateral relations due to the powerful nature of their bond that transcends even such fundamental discords.

For decades, the Arab states and the Palestinians have resented the US's one-sided support, blaming successive American administrations for having neglected the Palestinians to the detriment of their national aspiration for statehood. There is no doubt that the US's consistent support of Israel made it extremely difficult to be an honest broker; nevertheless, the Palestinians have had no choice but to cooperate with the US as a go-between negotiator if for no other reason than the US is the only country that can exert any influence on Israel to make certain concessions.

Fundamentally, by being the ultimate defender of Israel, the US has inadvertently become Israel's enabler, specifically because the US has hardly ever taken any political or economic measure against Israel and has not even slowed the delivery of weapons. This military support prevented Israel's enemies from attacking Israel at their whims, while politically, the US has provided Israel with a political shield in any international forum critical of Israel, especially the UNSC.

The US Policy Failure Toward Israel

The Israel-Hamas war has exposed the US policy failure toward Israel, as coming to Israel's support by providing an array of weapons, intelligence, and political cover while objecting to a long ceasefire made the Biden administration complicit to the unfolding horror

Israel unleashed against the Palestinians in Gaza. No one can ignore the fact that it is American jet fighters and American-made bombs that have inflicted such massive death and destruction. The death toll has exceeded 30,000, including nearly 20,000 women and children who were killed as a result of these bombings,[30] while laying half of Gaza in ruin. Nevertheless, the Biden administration continued to support Israel militarily while still providing it time and again with political cover, especially at the UNSC.

Reevaluation of US-Israel Relations

Whereas the US should continue to guarantee Israel's national security, this must no longer translate to giving Israel *carte blanche* to do as it pleases. The Israel-Hamas war has shown that the US's past policies toward Israel have, in fact, harmed Israel in that it allowed it to pursue policies and strategies against the Palestinians that are as detrimental to Israel itself as to the Palestinians.

For example, by not pressuring Israel to stop the building of settlements, which is illegal by international law and which Israel conveniently ignored, the US made it extremely difficult to find a solution to the settlement problem, making the establishment of a Palestinian state on a contiguous land mass extremely difficult while making the conflict ever more intractable. By allowing the occupation to persist for 57 years in the name of national security, the US became complicit to Israel's false claim that the occupation served Israel's national security.

The US Must Save Israel from Itself

The US must now translate its verbal opposition to the occupation into practical steps to bring an end to the occupation. The US must first make it absolutely clear that *Israel's greatest enemy* and threat

---

30 As of February 29, 2024, 30,035 Palestinians in Gaza have been killed since October 7, 2023, 58 to 70 percent of whom are women and children. See Aya Batrawy, "Gaza's death toll now exceeds 30,000. Here's why it's an incomplete count," *NPR*, February 29, 2024, https://www.npr.org/2024/02/29/1234159514/gaza-death-toll-30000-palestinians-israel-hamas-war.

to its national security is not Iran or Hezbollah, Hamas or Islamic Jihad, or any other foreign power or terrorist organization—*it is the occupation.* The US will defend Israel from any external power, but it cannot defend it from within. The occupation is eroding Israel's moral standing, debasing Jewish values that shielded the Jews for millennia, destroying its social fabric, consuming much of its financial and human resources, and isolating it from the international community. The worst of all is that it is poisoning the minds of Israel's youth against the Palestinians. Instead of inculcating them to grow up in peace, amity, and friendship with their immediate neighbors, they are turning them to hate and distrust the Palestinians while preparing them for the next war.

The US has inadvertently supported the occupation by doing little other than occasionally speaking against it, and in so doing, it has undermined rather than strengthened Israel's national security. Thus, being the ultimate defender of Israel, the US often finds itself drawn directly into the Israeli-Palestinian conflict and becomes mired in a conflagration not of its own choice. Because of this, the US has every right to demand that the Israeli government share its ultimate objective in connection with the Palestinians. If the current or any future Israeli government does not commit to a two-state solution, which is inconsistent with the US position, then the US should make it clear that it will take any measures deemed appropriate to end the Israeli occupation, which may include unilateral recognition of a Palestinian state, and taking stern measures to prevent Israel from further expansion of existing and building of new settlements.

The US must also be abundantly clear to the Palestinians that while the US will exert pressure on Israel to make the necessary concessions toward ending the occupation, the Palestinians must demonstrate that they are ready and willing to make the required concessions toward that end. The PA must show in practical terms that they are negotiating in good faith and will remain relentless until they reach a mutually agreed-upon solution with Israel.

Hamas's barbaric attack on October 7th and Israel's unprecedented invasion that destroyed half of Gaza and inflicted a horrific death toll has ironically created a new paradigm the Biden administration cannot afford not to take advantage of. It is time for President Biden, who has demonstrated in words and deeds the US's unshakable commitment to Israel's national security and his support of a two-state solution, to act on his promises and literally save Israel from itself.

There are measures that the US can take unilaterally, and it is also in a position to make specific demands from both Israelis and Palestinians and seek a breakthrough from the tragic breakdown that will bring the Israeli-Palestinian conflict to a close.

Creating a New Political Horizon

As a president highly seasoned in international affairs, Biden understands the pitfalls of a long and protracted conflict. Ending the war in Afghanistan provided him a glaring and painful example of how much can go wrong, yet he was still right and courageous to finally end it. He can demonstrate the same courage and leadership by changing the course of the Israeli-Palestinian conflict, which will eventually lead to peaceful coexistence based on a two-state solution.

There are those who rightfully make the argument that in an election year, President Biden may choose not to go this route out of fear that such a major initiative may fail and would adversely affect the outcome of the election. I do not subscribe to this argument for two reasons: first, the president will make it clear that he does not expect to reach a final agreement this year and will continue to work on it during his second term. Second, he has nothing to lose and will be credited for taking an initiative that none of his predecessors dared to take. This is where courage, vision, and leadership matter. But then, even if President Biden is not reelected, his successor (whoever that might be, including Trump, and regardless of his disdain toward Biden) would not want to squander such a historic breakthrough. He would certainly try to finalize what Biden has started and score a huge foreign policy triumph by taking credit for realizing something of such a historic magnitude.

Others argue that these are the worst times and conditions and the least conducive environment to discussing a two-state solution when it has eluded many interlocutors for decades under far more favorable political and security environments. I beg to differ because, as it has been said time and again since October 7th, Hamas' attack and Israel's retaliation are extraordinary both in scope and implication, making both sides realize that it is impossible to return to the *status quo that existed before October 7th*, which was not sustainable in the first place.

There are three reasons why it will be impossible to go back to the pre-October 7th status quo. First, under no circumstances, be that under an extreme government like the current one or a centrist government, will Israel allow Hamas to reconstitute itself in Gaza unless Hamas accepts a two-state solution, modifies its charter accordingly, and ends all instigation of violence. This is a tall order, but it cannot be ruled out, especially as the same was said about the PLO and given Hamas' choice between political survival or death. Two, the Arab states have started distancing themselves from the Palestinian issue by normalizing relations with Israel, which has not been the case any time before, even during the periods of Rabin and Peres.

This trend of further normalization of relations between Israel and other Arab countries will continue if the Palestinians resist entering into good-faith negotiations with the express purpose of reaching a two-state solution. Certainly, a different kind of status quo may evolve. Still, even under the drastically changing conditions at the present time, there is absolutely no way that there will be a new status quo that is worse than that which existed before October 7th.

Third, it is important to note here that the United States in particular, with the support of the EU and other Western powers, are now more determined than ever that the Israeli-Palestinian conflict must come to an end. As we are witnessing presently, the US is slowly being drawn into the conflict, which is dramatically affecting its geostrategic position and interests in the Middle East and alienating many Arab countries allied with the US. Furthermore, the US wants to avoid almost at all costs being further mired in the conflict, which is severely eroding its moral standing and what's left of its impartiality in the eyes of the Arab states and especially the Palestinians.

Moreover, how many more years or decades will we have to wait, and how much more death and destruction will both sides have to endure, before the right time comes? At no time before has the prospect of an Arab-Israeli peace been so realistic and doable, as was demonstrated by the Abraham Accords and Saudi Arabia's readiness to normalize relations with Israel.

Those who suggest that the political environment for a solution to the Israeli-Palestinian conflict was more positive between 1967 and 1973 ignore the fact that, at the time, the Palestinians were still committed to rejecting Israel's existence completely. That position changed in 1994, when Israel and the Palestinians reached an agreement in Oslo. The environment has continued to change since then on the international scene; the State of Palestine has had Observer Status at the United Nations since 2012. Moreover, as stated earlier, what existed 50 years ago is no longer relevant to the conditions today.

I do not see a scenario whereby Hamas, Islamic Jihad, or any other extremist Palestinian group will be able to reconstitute itself, govern Gaza, and undertake another vicious attack along the lines of October 7th. This will be nothing short of suicide, as we have seen from Israel's retaliation. In the wake of the Second Intifada, Israel went to the West Bank and inflicted massive damage. Ever since, Fatah has talked about a two-state solution. In fact, it was Netanyahu, starting in 1996 when he became prime minister, who was determined to scuttle the Oslo Accords, stating publicly that without his objection, a Palestinian state would have been created years ago.[lxxx]

Finally, the revolutionary change that has permeated the conflict raised the momentous question: where do we go from here? I challenge anyone to show me an alternative to ending the bloody 76-year-old Israeli-Palestinian conflict peacefully and sustainably that is not based on a two-state solution.

A HISTORIC POINT OF DEPARTURE

Unlike any peace initiative in the past, the US and Saudi Arabia must now abandon the conventional approaches to peace by *directly addressing the Israeli and Palestinian publics* instead of engaging in back-channel diplomacy or negotiating behind closed doors. The shock of October 7th and Israel's unparalleled retaliation warrants, just the same, a shockingly new approach to peace-making because the conventional approach has not only failed in the past but minimizes the gravity of what happened. More importantly, since addressing the public directly carries major political risks to the US and Saudi Arabia, by taking such a risk, they are demonstrating how high the stakes are and their determination to *seize the unprecedented opportunity* for a breakthrough while making their *proposed framework far more credible*. It is time for President Biden especially to abandon the US's traditional approach to Israeli-Palestinian peacemaking. Instead, he must seize the unprecedented opportunity, though created under tragic circumstances, as a historic point of departure by adopting a new strategy with Saudi Arabia, Jordan, and Egypt, that will bring closure to the Israeli-Palestinian conflict.

A Joint Statement by US President Biden, Saudi Crown Prince Mohammed bin Salman,[31] Jordan's King Abdallah, and Egypt's President Sisi

To introduce a departure of historic magnitude from previous peacemaking attempts, the US, Saudi Arabia, Jordan, and Egypt should make a historic joint statement, going over the heads of Netanyahu and his government as well as the Palestinian leadership,

---

31 Let me preface this by addressing the argument that Saudi Crown Prince Mohammed bin Salman has committed egregious human rights violations, which makes him unfit to play such a role. Given, however, that Saudi Arabia's role is central in effectuating Israeli-Palestinian peace and saving the lives of tens of thousands of Israelis and Palestinians and untold destruction in any future potential violent hostilities which are certain to come, his involvement is morally justifiable. Saudi Arabia's involvement in Israeli-Palestinian negotiations does not preclude the US and other Western powers from pressing the Crown Prince on human rights within the Kingdom separately.

about ending the Israeli-Palestinian conflict based on a two-state solution and its far-reaching regional implications. The idea here is to influence public opinion, as Israeli and Palestinian leaders alike are entrenched in their views and unwilling to listen to their public. This could occur alongside a referendum, along the lines of Northern Ireland—where, in that scenario, the political parties were fiercely committed to resistance and conflict, while the ordinary people on both sides of the conflict were tired and wanted peace with their neighbors. Although the language may vary, the joint public statement should be along the following lines:

> "After 76 years of heart-wrenching conflict between Israelis and Palestinians that claimed the lives of tens of thousands and inflicted untold destruction, it is time for you to face the truth: Seventy-six years have only deepened your conflict while exacting ever more blood and treasure from both of you. You coexist now, however precariously, and will continue to coexist indefinitely in one form or another. The recent tragic events have painfully demonstrated that the status quo was never sustainable, and the need for a solution has never been more urgent than now. Inaction will only lead to more catastrophic losses that must be avoided.
>
> We know that there are many conflicting and very difficult issues between you that must be resolved. Although the war in Gaza will end sooner than later, the violence in the West Bank is escalating, and it must be arrested before it explodes, which would make the prospective resolution to the conflict and reconciliation even more difficult.
>
> Nothing, though, will prevent you from solving the many differing issues if you are only willing to *come to terms with each other's inescapable reality*

and recognize that both of you have an inalienable right to an independent state of your own. Every Israeli should remember that there will be no circumstance under which the Palestinians will ever give up their right to statehood, without which Israel will not know a day of peace. Every Palestinian must understand that Israel is here to stay, and any power that attempts to dislodge it will do so at their peril.

Hence, peaceful coexistence is the only viable option. The alternative is the continuation of violence and mounting death and destruction while poisoning four more generations and readying them for the next war instead of striving for a promising future—a future where you can use your combined ingenuity and resourcefulness, flourish and grow together, and usher in a renaissance the region has never seen before. This is not delusional thinking on our part. Now, you have an unrivaled occasion to march forward with a common destiny. Nothing will impede you on your journey to peace and brotherhood as the common descendants of Abraham if you only will it.

The US, Saudi Arabia, Egypt, and Jordan, with other willing partners, stand ready to assist you in every way to facilitate peace negotiations with the objective of reaching a comprehensive peace agreement based on a two-state solution."

This joint statement should be accompanied by a full action plan encompassing all of the necessary provisions for a sustainable peace agreement based on a two-state solution.

First, as soon as the guns fall silent in Gaza and a transitional framework is in place and functioning, Saudi Arabia will enter into direct negotiations with Israel for the purpose of normalizing relations in all aspects and dimensions, and it will urge every Arab and Muslim state to recognize Israel in the spirit of the Arab Peace Initiative. This would offer a huge incentive to all Israelis regardless of their political leaning. As I said earlier, though, the process of normalization between Israel and Saudi Arabia will have to correspond to the progress made at the negotiating table between Israelis and Palestinians.

Second, the US will be ready to provide a security umbrella to all the countries in the region that are at peace with Israel. This will be in the form of a mutual defense treaty or any other joint security arrangement deemed desirable by the countries involved. This will be in line with the Saudis' requirement of a security guarantee from the US as a prerequisite to the normalization of relations with Israel. In addition, the US will be willing to provide military equipment tailored to the specific needs of each individual country.

Third, the negotiations will be conducted face-to-face between the newly-elected representatives of the Israeli government and the Palestinian Authority and will be monitored by American, Saudi, Jordanian, Egyptian, and EU representatives. Their role will be to facilitate the negotiating process and assist in mitigating differences between the two sides as they arise.

Fourth, to demonstrate its unshakable commitment to a two-state solution, the US will reopen its consulate in East Jerusalem to service the Palestinian population (this move will not prejudice the final status of Jerusalem) and will invite the Palestinian Authority to reestablish the Palestinian mission in Washington, D.C. Taking these steps will dramatically enhance, in the eyes of the Palestinians, the US commitment to a two-state solution, provided, of course, that they negotiate in good faith in order to reach an agreement to that end.

Fifth, the US and Saudi Arabia will provide, along with other countries, substantial financial assistance to rebuild Gaza and undertake major development projects in the West Bank. The economic aid will be provided on a continuing basis, allowing for the employment of tens of thousands of workers in all sectors of the economy, opening the door for thousands of youths to acquire higher education and professions and, together, will invariably raise the living standards of the communities at large.

Sixth, given the deeply rooted hatred and distrust and the overall poisonous atmosphere between Israelis and Palestinians, a process of reconciliation between the two sides must begin immediately. To that end, a commission composed of Israelis and Palestinians, aided by representatives of the US, the EU, Saudi Arabia, Egypt, and Jordan, will focus on the development of such a process that will include people-to-people and government-to-government measures and interaction to mitigate this intense ill-feeling and arrest the violence between them.

Seventh, although it is in the interest of Israel and the Palestinians to enter into good-faith peace negotiations, their refusal to do so will compel the United States to take action. Although the US will continue to guarantee Israel's national security, it will no longer provide blanket political cover to Israel, namely at the United Nations and any other forum where the US exerts significant political sway. The Palestinians will also stand to lose American economic assistance, as well as Arab political cover.

Eighth, six different negotiating teams will be established, four of which will focus on the main conflicting issues: national security, where full collaboration on all security matters is in place; the Palestinian refugees, which will have to be resolved based on resettlement and/or compensation; the Israeli settlements, which will have to be settled largely based on land swaps; and the future of Jerusalem, where the city will remain united while maintaining Jordan's custodianship over the Muslim holy shrines. The fifth team will focus on economic development, and the sixth will focus on social reconciliation.

A future Palestinian state will be independent, and ideally it should be democratic, but regardless, it will have to adhere to any agreement made between it and Israel. The territory of such an independent state would include all of Gaza and 93-94 percent of the West Bank. The six to seven percent remaining of the territories will be land swaps to accommodate for the Israeli settlements that cannot be relocated, specifically those in the three blocks along the 1967 border.

US Measures Needed to Advance the Peace Process

Given that Biden is on record supporting the two-state solution, he can immediately take several unilateral measures to convey to Israel and the Palestinians where his administration stands. Although such measures will certainly be welcomed by the Palestinians and may irk the Israelis, ultimately, they will serve the Israelis as much, if not more, than the Palestinians. These specific steps that Biden can unilaterally take will help lay the groundwork for a future substantive Israeli-Palestinian peace negotiation that could lead to a resolution of the conflict. In addition, restoring normal relations between the US and the Palestinians will give the Palestinians a sense of validation that would, in fact, soften their position and better prepare them to enter into serious negotiations in the context of confederation.

Biden's Requirements from the Palestinians

Biden should require the Palestinians to take numerous steps to demonstrate their commitment to a peaceful solution. This includes restating Israel's right to exist as an independent state, ending any and all forms of incitement against Israel, fully collaborating with Israel on all security matters, providing no protection to any violent Palestinian extremist, preventing any act of violence against Israelis in the West Bank, and ending any and all acrimonious public narratives against Israel.

New Parliamentary and Presidential Elections

Given that no election has been held by the Palestinians in over 20 years, Biden should demand that the Palestinian Authority establish an ironclad date for general and presidential elections. The elections should be monitored by international observers to ensure that they are free and fair, and all those seeking high office must publicly disavow the use of violence for political gains, recognize Israel's right to exist, and commit themselves to accepting the outcome of the elections. The Palestinians are in desperate need of new leadership untainted by corruption and not wedded to prior hard positions that left no room for compromises.

Israel must allow the Palestinians residing in East Jerusalem (who are not eligible to vote in Israeli national elections) to vote or be elected in any future Palestinian elections, a situation Israel has thus far refused to permit as allowing them to vote in Palestinian elections would be a tacit acknowledgment of Palestinian claims over East Jerusalem.

Biden's Requirements from Israel

Regardless of how compliant the Palestinians might be in meeting Biden's demands, they will not advance the reconciliation process unless Israel also takes certain measures on which Biden must insist to stabilize the Israeli-Palestinian relationship. In particular, Biden should require Israel not to act in any manner that would justifiably provoke the Palestinians.

Ending Any Annexation of Palestinian Lands

Biden should require Israel not to annex another inch of Palestinian land necessary for the creation of a viable independent Palestinian state. Israel must also end the practice of evicting Palestinians from their homes in any part of the West Bank, especially from East Jerusalem. Eviction is perceived by Palestinians as a highly egregious act that is intended to force the Palestinians out and replace them with Israeli Jews to change the demographic makeup of the city.

Freezing the Building of New and Legalizing Illegal Settlements

Perhaps there is no greater contentious and troubling concern for the Palestinians than the building of settlements. President Biden should make it clear to the Israeli government that it must freeze building new, expanding existing, and legalizing illegal settlements. Taken together, Israel's adherence to these requirements will help foster a calm atmosphere between Israel and the Palestinians, which is critical to a process of reconciliation.

Demanding that Israel Respect the Palestinians' Human Rights

Israel must immediately end any and all cruel practices, including night raids that terrify the Palestinians, especially children, uprooting olive trees, freezing Israeli settlement growth, ending the legalization of illegal settlements, stopping house demolitions, limiting the incarceration period of Palestinians accused of violent acts to no more than a month without charges, reducing security checkpoints to allow the Palestinians freer movement, and gradually releasing Palestinian prisoners who have no blood on their hands.

Cracking Down on the Settlers' Attacks on the Palestinians

Given that Israel cannot officially annex Palestine territory, it has allowed the settlers to do their sinister work to force the Palestinians to leave their land, which is one of the most egregious acts that has been condoned and even encouraged, especially by the current Netanyahu government. Settlers attacking Palestinian citizens has become routine. They have made it a daily practice to intimidate, threaten, and often physically attack and even kill innocent Palestinians. Confiscating their farmland, preventing them from grazing on their own land, and poisoning their water wells became a pastime, forcing many families to flee the land they had been living on, which was also their main source of livelihood. The Biden administration must demand the immediate cessation of such gross human rights violations.

PROCESS OF RECONCILIATION

Persuading both sides in the Israeli-Palestinian conflict that it's the right time to seek a resolution is challenging. Still, there are some approaches that can change the mindset. Both Israel and the Palestinians must engage in a process of reconciliation, which will bring about a gradual end to the Israeli-Palestinian conflict. Indeed, given the fact that Israelis and Palestinians have been estranged from one another, especially since the Second Intifada in 2000, and are profoundly distrustful of one another, *a process of reconciliation through joint government-to-government and people-to-people activities is essential.* The process of reconciliation is extremely critical to the majority of Israelis who do not believe that the Palestinians will ever accept Israel as an independent state and agree to coexist with it peacefully. To be sure, a process of reconciliation will also allow for a critical psychological shift in the attitude toward each other, which is central to changing their political and ideological beliefs.

I maintain that this is the most critical aspect that will make or break the prospect of permanently ending the Israeli-Palestinian conflict based on a two-state solution under the umbrella of confederation. A process of reconciliation consisting of multiple activities that must run simultaneously is *central* in order to *gradually mitigate the deep animosity and distrust between the two sides over time*, which cannot simply be overcome at the negotiating table.

This approach is consistent with the decade-long advocacy work by the Alliance for Middle East Peace, an umbrella organization of over 100 groups working in both Israel and the Palestinian territories. In December 2020, the US Congress approved a relief package of $250 million allocated for Israeli-Palestinian peacebuilding efforts specifically to expand people-to-people programs. Needless to say, this is an extremely important first step, and it must be substantially expanded over time. Any effort to reconcile between two adversaries could change the dynamic of the conflict, and this is where the US, the EU led by Germany, and the Arab States led by

Saudi Arabia can steer the process toward a two-state solution. The parties involved must insist on the following measures.

Government-to-government Measures

i) **Halting the mutually acrimonious public narrative:** Israeli and Palestinian leaders must stop their acrimonious public narratives against each other. This is perhaps the most critical point that must be addressed. Rather than preparing the public for the inevitability of peace and engaging in constructive public dialogue, they have been poisoning the political atmosphere and setting one side against the other, creating the perception that peace is an illusion and that the differences between them are irreconcilable. The promulgation of such charges and countercharges adversely impacts the general mindsets of their respective publics and creates the perception among young and old alike that peaceful coexistence is impossible. Reconciliation must begin first by changing the public narrative, which connotes a process of mutual acceptance between ordinary Israelis and Palestinians, and at the highest level.

ii) **Establishing an economic relationship:** Developing a strong economic relationship between Israel and the Palestinians is central because without it, no process of reconciliation will work. Other than trade between the two sides, Israeli investors should be encouraged to invest in various business enterprises in the future Palestinian state, which would provide a significant amount of employment for Palestinians, who have among the highest unemployment rates in the world.[32] Israel can also help the Palestinians create and manage large projects, for example, in housing, healthcare centers, schools, and infrastructure, as well as sustainable development projects. Economic exchanges, investment, and devel-

---

32 Total Palestinian unemployment as of 2019 is 25.3 percent—14.6 percent in the West Bank and a staggering 45.2 percent in Gaza, with women and youth bearing the greatest burden in both areas (International Labour Organization 2020).

opment will foster a very close relationship between the two sides, and the benefits can be reaped within a relatively short period of time. Neither side, especially the Palestinians, would want to risk losing such tangible benefits after such an exchange is developed from which they greatly benefit.

iii) **Modifying school textbooks:** It is necessary for both sides to modify school textbooks to reflect an objectively more accurate and less biased historical account throughout their educational institutions. This is particularly a sore point for the Israelis, as the Palestinians' history books refer to Israel only as an occupying power. The 1967 borders are not delineated in geography books, and on Palestinian maps, the state of Palestine covers what is currently Israel, the West Bank, and Gaza. Although a few years ago Israel modified some of its textbooks, current textbooks deny Israel's role in precipitating the Palestinian refugee problem and disseminate other inaccurate historic accounts. The contextual environment in schools and all institutions and any social settings in which they come in contact can significantly reinforce the fact that their coexistence is irreversible.

iv) **Developing integrated schools:** Educational divisions have a long-lasting impact on students of every background, both socially and educationally—the budget for the average Jewish student is 78 to 88 percent higher than for an Arab student, and Arabs go on to be underrepresented in universities.[lxxxi] In Israel itself, rarely do Jewish and Arab students attend the same schools, which would otherwise be the ideal place for children of different backgrounds to meet and interact with each other and learn that they are not enemies but neighbors. Integrated schools, like Hagar and Hand in Hand, are essential in fostering ideas and positive attitudes toward coexistence from a young age and should be expanded upon in Israel proper. These schools teach classes bilingually, in both Arabic and Hebrew, which is critical as language is the first step in creating a shared understanding.

While this does not address the need for Palestinian children in the West Bank and Gaza to meet and interact with their Israeli counterparts, the expansion of such schools will build understanding among Israelis of every background and could be expanded under conditions of peace to areas in the West Bank where settlers live side-by-side Palestinians. Even in segregated schools, understanding can be expanded upon. In both Israeli and Palestinian schools, language learning should be compulsory—Arabic for Israeli students and Hebrew for Palestinian students. Language is more than a means by which to communicate; it represents an entire culture. Indeed, even Hamas recognizes that learning Hebrew is essential to "understanding the enemy," and has expanded Hebrew-language classes for Gazan children.[lxxxii]

v) **Taking no provocative action:** The US should insist that the PA not go to the International Criminal Court (ICC) to charge Israel with crimes against humanity or seek further UNSC resolutions, be that against the settlements or in favor of recognition. Such a step would have little, if any, practical effect on Israel and it would only enrage the Israelis as they see it as a form of incitement, which will only further harden their position. Moreover, the mere threat of seeking justice through the ICC will also send the wrong message to the Palestinian public at large that relations with Israel are worsening rather than improving, which will have an adverse psychological effect and make reconciliation ever more difficult.

In return, the US should heavily lean on Israel to take a number of conciliatory measures to demonstrate its willingness to work with the Palestinians in order to create a more positive atmosphere on which to build mutual trust. First, Israel could release over a period of a few months hundreds of Palestinian prisoners who are in prison for non-violent crimes. Second, Israel can facilitate the issuance of building permits to the Palestinians to provide them with the sense that they are free to strike deep roots in their future state. Third, Israel must stop the practice of night raids, except under special circumstances and only *with the presence of the Palestin-*

ians' own internal security. Fourth, restrictions over the movement of Palestinians within the West Bank should be eased to signal to ordinary Palestinians that an end to the occupation is in the offing and demonstrate what peace could usher in once both sides come to terms with one another. Finally, Israel must stop any settlement expansion beyond the areas denoted earlier, which are envisioned to be part of a potential land swap.

vi) Maintaining security cooperation: Israel should not only continue to work together with the Palestinians' internal security service, but further augment future cooperation on all security matters. This will help solidify the overall security situation and pave the way for even more extensive joint operations following the establishment of a Palestinian state. It should be noted that some current and future violent clashes will be unavoidable and are likely to intensify further as long as the Palestinians see no hope for a better future and the Israelis continue to feel vulnerable about their national security. Alleviating that sense of concern both psychologically and practically has been and remains central to successful peace talks.

The US must insist that both sides refrain from using violence and embrace the late Yitzhak Rabin's mantra: "Fight terrorism as if there is no peace process; pursue peace as if there is no terrorism." Unfortunately, both sides have historically resorted to violence as the first choice rather than as a last resort. This approach has proven its futility over time as 76 years later, little or no improvement has been made in the way they perceive and treat each other. There will always be certain elements on both sides who are determined to destroy any prospect for peace, either because of their deep, ideologically uncompromising bent, or because they have and continue to benefit financially from the continuing conflict. In the context of the overall Israeli-Palestinian conflict, fortunately, these groups are marginal and will not succeed in undermining the peace process. Only a united front from within both camps will blunt the efforts by violent extremists to sabotage the negotiations.

vii) **Establishing healthcare institutions:** Being that Israel is one of the leading countries in the area of healthcare and medical breakthroughs, it can certainly aid the Palestinians in building clinics and hospitals in the Palestinian state while providing medical training to hundreds of Palestinians. This includes doctors, nurses, and medical technicians. In addition, the Israeli government can facilitate access to Israeli hospitals for Palestinians who need advanced treatment not currently available in Palestinian hospitals. Given that healthcare affects everyone in one form or another, Israel's regular assistance to the Palestinians in this crucial area will go a long way toward reconciliation and strongly mitigate the distrust between the two sides.

viii) **Housing projects:** Before any other steps, Israel's past policy of not issuing building permits for Palestinians in Area C and East Jerusalem must end immediately. Even when permits have been announced, such as the approval of 700 permits in 2019, they are rarely issued in reality.[lxxxiii] Israel can aid the Palestinian government in meeting the growing demand for housing, especially for Palestinian refugees who choose to relocate from refugee camps outside Palestine to the West Bank and internally displaced Palestinians who need to resettle in new communities. Israel can help the Palestinian government build new communities using prefabricated housing within months. In addition, as a gesture of goodwill, if and when Israeli settlers from small settlements are relocated, Israel can turn over housing in those areas to Palestinians by agreement between the two sides.

People-to-people Measures

As the above measures are taken, people-to-people interaction becomes a natural process conducted in a constantly improving atmosphere. The following measures, which are being pursued today on a small scale, need to be employed much more widely in a cohesive and consistent manner to create a new political and social environment that would support the negotiating process. The

Israelis and the Palestinians must be challenged and pressured to implement them if they are truthfully seeking to end the conflict.

i) **Mutual visitation**: The Israeli government and the Palestinian Authority must agree to allow mutual visitation. Concerns over security can certainly be adequately addressed; Israel is in a perfect position to institute background checks in advance, along the lines of security procedures in airports, to prevent the infiltration of Islamic radicals and weapons. It is hard to exaggerate the value of such visits when ordinary Israelis and Palestinians meet in their respective places of residence to share experiences and understand each other's grievances and concerns, as many have often discovered that their shared interests and aspirations are far greater than their differences.

ii) **Women's activism**: Activism by Israeli and Palestinian women can be a very important part of the reconciliation process. Israeli and Palestinian women should use their formidable power to demand that their respective leaders end the conflict. Women have far greater sway than men if they join forces, engage in peaceful demonstrations, and remain consistent with the message to cease all forms of violence. The role of women in ending the conflict in Northern Ireland and throughout the wars in the Balkans offers a vivid picture of how women can impact the course of events.

iii) **Joint sporting events**: Sports are incredibly useful in building camaraderie and friendship between the two sides, whether competing against each other or as part of a joint team. Israeli and Palestinian football, basketball, and other sports teams can meet alternately in Israel and Palestine to train, compete, and develop personal relationships. Joint Israeli-Palestinian teams, such as existing youth teams in basketball and football, create an environment where children from both backgrounds learn to work together toward a common goal. For girls especially, this can create an environment where girls of all religious backgrounds can be free and comfortable, even in a cross-cultural environment. This type of activity allows them to have a much better sense of who the other is. They begin to view one another as ordinary individuals who cheer the generous spirit of the game that they are playing together, *where the victory is the game itself, not the final score.*

iv) **Student interaction**: Palestinian and Israeli students (from primary school through university) should connect and mingle with one another and talk about their aspirations and hopes for the future. No Israeli or Palestinian child should continue to be fed poisonous ideas that the other is a mortal foe or anything less than human. A Palestinian youth should not view every Israeli as a soldier with a gun, and conversely, no Israeli youth should view every Palestinian as a terrorist. On the contrary, Israeli and Palestinian youth should be taught that they are destined to peacefully coexist and be encouraged to use social media to communicate with each other, as the future rests in their hands.

v) **Art exhibitions**: Scores of Israeli and Palestinian artists have never met or delved into each other's feelings and mindsets to see how their works reflect their lives. Joint exhibitions should take place both in Israel and Palestine, touring several cities to allow people young and old to see and feel what the other is trying to express. These cultural exchanges can expand to include music festivals, theater performances, and other forms of art.

vi) **Public discourse**: Universities, think tanks, and other learning institutions should organize roundtable discussions. The participants should consist of qualified Israelis and Palestinians with varied academic and personal experiences who enjoy respect in their field, are independent thinkers, *hold no formal position* in their respective governments, and have thorough knowledge of the conflicting issues. For example, they can discuss how both sides can remove the barriers to make coexistence not only inevitable but desirable. These roundtable discussions should include other topics related to regional and international issues in order to learn from each other's perspectives on how to assess a certain conflict or a dispute between other nations. Such small roundtable discussions can be disseminated online to millions of people, including Israelis and Palestinians, instantly.

vii) Interfaith gatherings: Given the fact that Jerusalem is at the heart of the three Abrahamic religions, arranging interfaith discussions consisting of religious scholars, imams, rabbis, and priests is critical. The participants can address issues of concern and interest to the three religions. For example, in addressing the future of Jerusalem, even though Jerusalem may well become the capital of two states, debating other possibilities is critical if for no other reason but to demonstrate why other options may not work. These gatherings can extend beyond scholarly discussions as well. Religious leaders such as rabbis and imams can organize interfaith Seders and iftars, where community members of every religion can come together and learn about each other's religion in an atmosphere of celebration, not tension.

viii) Business partnerships: Business partnerships between Israelis and Palestinians will go a long way not only to foster economic relations in which both sides have a vested financial interest in which they want to succeed but also to nurture close personal relationships and trust. Such partnerships, which almost always require many employees, will allow Israeli and Palestinian employees to work together and take pride in their joint endeavors. For example, Israeli construction companies could partner with their Palestinian counterparts to undertake large joint projects, building infrastructure such as roads, bridges, and hospitals, among other projects.

ix) The role of the media: Instead of focusing almost solely on violence and acrimonious charges and counter-charges that make headlines, Israeli and Palestinian media should also be encouraged to report on positive developments between the two sides to inform the people that the bilateral relations are not all discouraging. For example, they can discuss ongoing trade, security, and health care cooperation, Palestinians studying in Israeli universities, et cetera. In this sense, the media should play a critical role and assume some responsibility in disseminating timely information about the need for public-to-public interactions. The media should publicize these events as they occur, and columnists and commentators should encourage more such activities. Moreover, Palestinian journalists should be free to report from Israel, and their Israeli counterparts should also be welcome to report from the Palestinian state. In addition, television and radio stations should invite Israelis and Palestinians to publicly discuss issues of concern and interest to both sides in a series of town hall-style discussions. Finally, the media can play a pivotal role in shaping bilateral Israeli-Palestinian relations, emphasizing the fact that the two peoples will be living indefinitely side-by-side, and that cooperation between them is imperative to their welfare and future well-being.

The failure of both sides to agree in the past to establish and be governed by the above rules of engagement clearly suggests that neither side negotiated in good faith. All influential powers—specifically the Biden administration with the strong support of Germany, Saudi Arabia, Jordan, and Egypt—must use their weight and influence to the maximum extent that Israelis and Palestinians accept the above rules if they want to achieve peace. Otherwise, any new peace talks will be nothing but an exercise in futility.

THE REGIONAL IMPLICATIONS

It is hard to exaggerate the regional implications if an Israeli-Palestinian peace is achieved that leads to normalization of relations between Israel and Saudi Arabia and subsequently to a comprehensive Arab-Israeli peace. To begin with, Israeli-Palestinian peace will dramatically reduce regional violence and substantially improve stability, while expanding the region's economic development and technological advancement.

Due to the firm Saudi requirement that the US offer a mutual defense treaty in exchange for Saudi Arabia's normalization of relations with Israel, the US can offer a security umbrella to all the countries that are at peace with Israel. While there is currently a *de facto* informal American security guarantee, this would formalize it. Such an alliance will create a crescent extending from the Gulf to the Mediterranean that includes Saudi Arabia, Bahrain, the United Arab Emirates, Kuwait, Oman, Qatar, Jordan, Palestine, Israel, and Egypt.

This security and economic alliance will also send an unmistakable message to Iran that although the purpose of the alliance is not to threaten Iran's security and governance, it is a warning that it's time for it to cease and desist its campaign to destabilize the region—a practice that Tehran has been engaged in through its surrogate militias in Iraq, Syria, Yemen, Lebanon, and Palestine with Hamas and Islamic Jihad, the so-called "axis of resistance." Such an alliance will allay Israel's concerns over Iran's nuclear program and its potential to produce nuclear weapons. It will also inhibit Russia's ambition to further expand its influence in the region. Moreover, such an alliance will put Tehran on notice that the US views Iran's ambition to oust the US from the Middle East as hostile and will no longer tolerate it.

Moreover, and more importantly, an Israeli-Palestinian peace will certainly pull the rug out from under Iran because Iran's opposition to Israel was mostly based on the fact that Israel has been denying the Palestinians a state of their own. But once they establish their own state, Iranian resistance to Israel will be weakened dramatically, if not fully collapse. This will also have serious implications on the Israeli mindset in terms of the Iranian threat.

ISRAEL MUST REMEMBER ITS MORAL VALUES

Israel must uphold its moral values and make every effort
to spare the lives of innocent Palestinians as it pursues
Hamas' destruction

Given that the Israel-Gaza war continues to rage as I write this book, I know that many more thousands of Palestinians and hundreds of Israeli soldiers will die before the war ends. Having witnessed the terrifying scenes of Hamas' onslaught and the unfolding horror of the Israeli invasion, I thought that I should conclude this book with a warning to the Israelis that notwithstanding Hamas' atrocities, Israel must uphold its Jewish values and climb back to the highest moral ground by not engaging in any further acts of revenge and retribution.

The unfathomable massacre of Israeli Jews by Hamas and its insatiable thirst for Jewish blood has rightfully evoked the most virulent condemnation from many corners of the world, including many Arab states. The call for revenge and retribution by many Israelis was an instinctive human reaction that can be justified in a moment of incomparable rage and devastation. In this case, the Israelis' reaction transcended Hamas' massacre because it brought to life memories from the Holocaust that the Jews foresworn to never let happen again. But it happened, though on a much smaller scale; the savagery and the cold-bloodedness that characterized Hamas' attack was reminiscent of the Holocaust, which is etched in the mind and soul of the Jews.

Israel's decision to crush Hamas as a political movement, destroy its infrastructure, and prevent it from reconstituting itself is necessary, and it should relentlessly be pursued with vigor. Under no circumstances and regardless of what the Jews have experienced, however, can the Israeli military justify any acts of revenge against innocent Palestinian men, women, and children who have nothing to do with Hamas' evil act.

None of the dead or injured Palestinian women and children were asked by Hamas' leaders whether they should go and massacre innocent Israelis at an unprecedented scale. Although Hamas knew full well the unimaginable price these ordinary Palestinians would end up paying, Hamas was more than willing to sacrifice their welfare and well-being as they have done over the years to serve their hollow ideology. They died by the tens of thousands as the sacrificial lamb on the altar of the most vicious beasts that roam the earth.

After more than six months of fighting that inflicted horrific death and destruction on Gaza and claimed the lives of more than 30,000, two-thirds of them women and children, while laying half of Gaza in utter ruin, one must ask the question: was there a strong element of revenge that contributed to this colossal human disaster? Tragically, the answer is YES. The role of the victim is deeply ingrained in the Jewish psyche, and the leap from being victim to victimizer is subconscious; acting on it is spontaneous. That said, the extent and the scope of the Israeli reaction calls into question whether or not Israeli soldiers have been engaged in acts of revenge beyond their legitimate right to self-defense.

When we see in real-time the destruction of one neighborhood after another, horrendously transcending any proportionality of collateral damage which is often unavoidable in a state of war, we see revenge and retribution.

When soldiers boast of serving in the most moral military force in the world but laugh and dance following the explosion and leveling of a residential building to the ground, killing dozens of civilians among one or two suspected Hamas fighters, it is not an act of self-defense, it is an act of vengeance that defies the logic of what is moral.

When the entire population of Gaza is facing "catastrophic levels of acute food insecurity"[33] and hundreds of children are dying from

33 According to the Integrated Food Security Phase Classification (IPC), Level 3, Crisis, is defined by acute malnutrition rates of ten to fifteen percent; the

curable illnesses because they could not receive the medical treat-ment and the medicine they need, it is an unforgivable crime the whole world is watching in real-time with revulsion and disdain.

When a majority of the Palestinians are forced to evacuate their homes with women and children, and the sick are forced to walk for miles with little or no rations, not knowing where they will sleep and where the next meal will come from, it is cruel and de-void of any moral culpability.

When an entire family is buried alive under the rubble of their building that collapsed over their heads, and they die a slow death before the rescuers and medical teams can save anyone, it is inhu-man and severely damages the high moral ground the Israeli army has proudly claimed.

More than 12,000 children have been killed in Gaza,[lxxxiv] includ-ing 258 babies who never had the chance to celebrate their first birthday.[lxxxv] Infants and toddlers are children just beginning to dis-cover the world. Can the barbaric and utterly condemnable attack by Hamas on October 7th justify or explain the horrific killing of innocents on this scale? How can any people who claim to cherish life, steal it away from so many completely innocent children, who had their entire lives ahead of them? The only true explanation for this is revenge—and the cycle of revenge will continue indefinitely.

Shortly after October 7th, I recall an interview with an Israeli sol-dier who said outright that he "needs his revenge." Does not that soldier, and everyone who thinks like him, realize that this is pre-cisely how Hamas was operating on October 7th? Is it not obvious that revenge, by its very nature, has no end? It is a mechanical and thoughtless response to injury that repeats itself until one party has

---

highest level 5, Famine, is categorized by at least 30 percent of children suffer-ing from acute malnutrition and a death rate of at least two per 10,000 each day. The IPC estimates that 50 percent of Gaza's population is at level 4, and one in four households are at level 5. See https://www.ipcinfo.org/ipc-coun try-analysis/details-map/en/c/1156749/?iso3=PSE for more information.

the moral strength and courage to say enough is enough—we will not go on slaughtering each other wholesale, exacting retribution on individuals who have committed no wrong, whose deaths are meant only to maximize the suffering of those who loved and cherished them.

Does not every Israeli mother realize that every Palestinian mother cares for their children with the same boundless love that they have for their own? Does Israel truly believe that a Palestinian infant has less value than an Israeli babe-in-arms? Can anyone truthfully believe that the moral response to having one's innocent loved ones killed is to kill more innocents? And on what scale? How many dead Palestinian children will it take to satiate the desire for revenge? There is no end, because no matter how many Palestinian children Israel kills it will not bring back to life a single one of those Israeli younglings that were killed on October 7th.

Israel is not honoring its dead by this slaughter and devastation, but just the opposite. It is disgracing the dead and themselves. Israel appears bent on demonstrating before the whole world that it has lost all sense of moral compass, proportionality, pity, and compassion. The Jewish people are better than this—it is they who taught us that to save one human life is to save the world. The deliberate shedding of innocent blood is and will always be an atrocious act of evil that can never be morally justified. And the time has come for Israel to bring an end to this retribution before it loses its soul and whatever moral sympathy the world had for the wrong it suffered over six months ago.

Prime Minister Netanyahu is justifying this collective punishment by dehumanizing the Palestinians, deeming them unworthy of humane treatment. He is waging a merciless campaign against innocent Palestinians who had nothing to do with Hamas' acts of terror. For Netanyahu, there is simply no moral equivalence. For him and many of his deplorable followers, the Palestinians are sub-humans, and their lives are unequal to those of Israeli Jews.

Israel will win this war—the question is, will it win it while adhering to Jewish moral values that have guided and ensured their survival throughout the centuries, or win it by leaving behind deep moral wounds that will be etched in memory and history books as one of Israel's darkest chapters? They must remember that just about every Arab country will quietly (and some even overtly) cheer the demise of Hamas, but they are and will continue to speak ever louder and clearer about their objection to the killing of innocent Palestinians, especially women and children, and they will scuttle any prospect of normalization of relations between Israel and other Arab states.

The dehumanization of Palestinians will come back to haunt the Israelis simply because the Palestinians have no other place to go. And whether they are ordinary human beings with hopes and aspirations or subhuman, Israel is stuck with them. And regardless of how the war will end, Israel will have to address the conflict with the Palestinians. The depth of the scars of the war will define the relationship for years to come.

As the death toll and destruction rise in Gaza by the minute, the initial overwhelming sympathy toward Israel's tragic losses has waned even among many of its friends. Indeed, once Israel loses its moral compass in dealing with the crisis, it will no longer be seen as the victim who rose from the ashes of the Holocaust and has every right to defend itself but the victimizer whose survival rests on the ashes of the Palestinians.

Israel's ultimate triumph rests on its ability to rise above the fray and adhere to the moral values on which the country was founded and which are the only pillars that can sustain it.

CONCLUSION

Since the beginning of the Israeli occupation in 1967, all peace negotiations have failed mainly because neither side was willing *to recognize the other's inalienable right* to live in an independent state of their own. Both sides missed numerous opportunities, allowing the extremists among them to usurp the political agenda and torpedo any efforts by moderates/realists on both sides to reach an agreement.

Every Israeli should remember that for the Palestinians, having a state of their own is the only acceptable solution. They will not continue to live in servitude; they want to be free; they want security, opportunities to grow and prosper, and a promising future. They will never succumb to the draconian rules of the occupier and will resist until they unshackle themselves of occupation.

Every Palestinian should also know that *there will be no independent Palestinian state* unless the Palestinians accept coexistence with Israel in peace and security. Israel has an inalienable right to exist as a Jewish state where all of its citizens, regardless of their ethnic background and religious affiliation, enjoy equal rights before the law.

Israelis and Palestinians ought to remember *that their co-existence is irrevocable.* They are either destined to grow, prosper, and live in peace together, or kill each other for another 100 years. The choice is theirs—to bequeath either life or death to generations to come.

There has never been a better time for the US to establish such a far-reaching regional order in the Middle East, the consequences of which will revolutionize regional security and economic developments and gradually bring an end to the decades-long strife. Millions are subjected to violence and deprivation while being robbed of their basic human right to live in peace and security.

President Biden must not miss this rare occasion, as he has already committed himself to a two-state solution, and now all forces are aligned not only to realize this goal but create a new regional alliance that will change the course of history of the Middle East for generations to come.

ALON BEN-MEIR

APPENDIX: CONFEDERATION

Given the geographic proximity and the intertwined relationship between Israel, Jordan, and the Palestinians, future cooperation and collaborations on political, economic, and security levels, as well as Jerusalem, become critically important between the three countries. For this reason, once an independent Palestinian state is established, it should be followed by the creation of an Israeli-Palestinian-Jordanian confederation that will work collaboratively but voluntarily on issues of mutual concern. Such a confederation will help sustain the Israeli-Palestinian peace agreement while enhancing their security and dramatically contribute to their prosperity and growth.

Confederations are defined as "voluntary associations of *independent states* that, to secure some common purpose, agree to certain limitations on their freedom of action and establish some joint machinery of consultation or deliberation [emphasis added]."[34]

What is important to emphasize about the concept of confederation is that the countries involved *maintain their independence,* and their collaboration on mutual issues of concern, though necessary, remains voluntary. The more they cooperate, however, the greater the benefit they engender and the more opportunities present themselves for further expansion of their collaborative efforts.

Such a confederation would join independent Israeli, Palestinian, and Jordanian states together on issues of common interest *that cannot be addressed but in full collaboration under the framework of confederation.* This includes the future status of Jerusalem, national security, the fate of the settlements, and the Palestinian refugees. Their previous failure to come to an agreement precipitated largely by contradictory national interests, historical narratives, and psychological impediments on these issues explains why the conflict became increasingly intractable. Both sides sought concessions to

---

34 As defined by *Encyclopedia Britannica.*

136

which the other could not acquiesce, driven by their failure to negotiate in good faith.

Now, new conditions have been created on the ground. However, *given the inevitability of coexistence, whether under hostile or peaceful conditions,* an agreement in principle on the establishment of a confederation from the onset as the ultimate goal could allow both sides to jointly resolve and manage the facts on the ground, which are not subject to a dramatic shift and are central to reaching a sustainable peace agreement.[35]

---

35 For further details about the concept of an Israeli-Palestinian-Jordanian confederation, see Alon Ben-Meir, "The Case for an Israeli-Palestinian-Jordanian Confederation: Why Now and How?"

Endnotes

i   Alon Ben-Meir, "Introduction to the Special Issue: Continued Israeli Occupation Is a Ticking Time Bomb," *World Affairs* 185, no. 4 (October 3, 2022): 650–75, https://doi.org/10.1177/00438200221128788.

ii "Why the Palestinian Group Hamas Launched an Attack on Israel? All to Know," *Al Jazeera*, October 9, 2023, https://www.aljazeera.com/news/2023/10/7/palestinian-group-hamas-launches-surprise-attack-on-israel-what-to-know.

iii John Gramlich, "What the data says about gun deaths in the U.S.," Pew Research Center, April 26, 2023, https://www.pewresearch.org/short-reads/2023/04/26/what-the-data-says-about-gun-deaths-in-the-u-s/.

iv Gil Hoffman and Tovah Lazaroff, "No Palestinian State under Bennett-Led Government, FM Says," *The Jerusalem Post*, August 20, 2021, https://www.jpost.com/israel-news/no-palestinian-state-under-bennett-led-government-lapid-says-677235.

v   Sigmund Freud, *The Future of an Illusion*, trans. Gregory C. Richter, ed. Todd Dufresne (Peterborough: Broadview Press, 2012), 93-94.

vi Freud, 93.

vii David Rabinowitz, "The Psychological Dimensions of the Israeli-Palestinian Conflict: The Role of Psychological Resistance," In correspondence with the author, Haifa, Israel, 2012, 2.

viii Alon Ben-Meir, "Does Israel's Right Cultivate a Permanent Enemy to Justify a Permanent Occupation?" *History News Network*, April 17, 2022, https://historynewsnetwork.org/article/182980.

ix UNRWA, "Palestine Refugees," United Nations Relief and Works Agency, accessed March 6, 2024, https://www.unrwa.org/palestine-refugees.

x   "Ben-Zvi Sees Population Exchange as Solution of Arab Refugee Problem," Jewish Telegraphic Agency, December 5, 1960, https://www.jta.org/archive/ben-zvi-sees-population-exchange-as-solution-of-arab-refugee-problem; and Yehouda Shenhav, "Arab Jews, Population Exchange, and the Palestinian Right of Return," in *Exile and Return: Pre-*

dicaments of Palestinians and Jews, ed. Ann M. Lesch and Ian S. Lustick (Philadelphia: University of Pennsylvania Press, 2008), 225-245.

xi "Despite EU Vow to End Incitement, Palestinian Textbooks Remain Unaltered – Report," *The Times of Israel*, January 30, 2022, https://www.timesofisrael.com/despite-eu-vow-to-end-incitement-palestin ian-textbooks-remain-unaltered-report/; and Or Kashti, "In Israeli Textbooks, the Palestinians Are All But Invisible," *Haaretz*, June 21, 2020, https://www.haaretz.com/israel-news/2020-06-21/ty-article/. premium/in-israeli-textbooks-the-palestinians-are-all-but-invisi ble/0000017f-f53a-d318-afff-f77b47ba0000.

xii Alain Badiou, *Polemics*, trans. Steve Corcoran (New York: Verso, 2012), 160.

xiii Alexander Joffe and Asaf Romirowsky, "The Politics of the Palestinian Right of Return," *Forbes*, February 24, 2014, https://www.forbes.com/sites/realspin/2014/02/24/the-politics-of-the-palestin ian-right-of-return/?sh=5eaab30c608b.

xiv "Likud Party Platform from the 15th Knesset," Webarchive.org, 1999, (accessed October 5, 2022), https://web.archive.org/web/2007093018 1442/https://www.knesset.gov.il/elections/knesset15/elikud_m. htm.

xv Cited in Jennifer Jefferis, *Hamas: Terrorism, Governance, and Its Future in Middle East Politics* (Santa Barbara, CA: Praeger, 2016); see also "The Covenant of the Islamic Resistance Movement," The Avalon Project, August 18, 1988 (accessed October 1, 2022), http://avalon.law. yale.edu/20th_century/hamas.asp.

xvi Terry Eagleton, *Ideology* (London: Verso, 1991), 2.

xvii Eagleton, 5.

xviii United Nations, "Khartoum Resolution," September 1, 1967, accessed October 2, 2022, https://www.un.org/unispal/document/au to-insert-193039/.

xix General Assembly Agenda Item 10, Declaration of Principles on Interim Self-Government Arrangements, A/48/486 (11 October 1993), available from https://peacemaker.un.org/israelopt-osloaccord93.

xx Dag Henrik Tuastad, "The Hudna: Hamas's Concept of a Long-term Ceasefire," PRIO Policy Brief, 9. Oslo: PRIO, 2010, https://www.prio.org/publications/7356.

xxi Alon Ben-Meir, "The Creation of a Palestinian State is Inescapable," *Jerusalem Post*, June 26, 2021, https://www.jpost.com/opinion/the-creation-of-a-palestinian-state-is-inescapable-opinion-672112.

xxii J.M. Bernstein, "The Harm of Rape, the Harm of Torture," in *Torture and Dignity: An Essay on Moral Injury* (Chicago, IL: Chicago University Press, 2015), 119, https://doi.org/10.7208/chicago/9780226266466.003.0004.

xxiii "Despite EU Vow to End Incitement, Palestinian Textbooks Remain Unaltered – Report."

xxiv Kashti.

xxv Herbert C. Kelman, "The Social Context of Torture: Policy Process and Authority Structure," in *The Politics of Pain: Torturers and Their Masters*, 19-34 (New York: Routledge, 2019), 29.

xxvi Kelman, 31.

xxvii Bernstein, 119.

xxviii Benjamin Netanyahu, "Text of PM Binyamin Netanyahu's speech to the US Congress," *Jerusalem Post*, May 24, 2011, accessed October 1, 2022, http://www.jpost.com/DiplomacyAndPolitics/Article.aspx?id=222056.

xxix Omar Shakir, "Raising the Alarm: Israel's All-Out Assault on Rights Defenders," Human Rights Watch, August 19, 2022, https://www.hrw.org/news/2022/08/19/raising-alarm-israels-all-out-assault-rights-defenders.

xxx "ISA Detains and Interrogates B'Tselem Field Researcher; B'Tselem: 'Disgraceful Arrest Aimed at Hampering the Work of a Human Rights Organization,'" B'Tselem, August 12, 2022, https://www.btselem.org/press_releases/20220812_isa_detains_and_interrogates_btselem_field_researcher.

xxxi Isabel Kershner, "Palestinian Leader Accused Israel of '50 Holocausts,'

Causing an Uproar," *New York Times*, August 17, 2022, https://www.nytimes.com/2022/08/17/world/middleeast/palestinian-leader-accused-israel-of-50-holocausts-causing-an-uproar.html.

xxxii "Poll Summary: Palestinian-Israeli Pulse," Palestinian Center for Policy and Survey Research, August 13, 2018, https://www.pcpsr.org/en/node/731.

xxxiii Scott B. Lasensky, "How to Help Palestinian Refugees Today," Jerusalem Center for Public Affairs, February 2, 2003, https://www.jcpa.org/jl/vp491.htm.

xxxiv "30 Years after Oslo – the Data That Shows How the Settlements Proliferated Following the Oslo Accords," Peace Now, September 11, 2023, https://peacenow.org.il/en/30-years-after-oslo-the-data-that-shows-how-the-settlements-proliferated-following-the-oslo-accords.

xxxv Clyde Haberman, "Shamir Is Said to Admit Plan to Stall Talks 'for 10 Years,'" *The New York Times*, June 27, 1992, https://www.nytimes.com/1992/06/27/world/shamir-is-said-to-admit-plan-to-stall-talks-for-10-years.html.

xxxvi Shaul Arieli and Nimrod Novik, "In West Bank Reality, Annexation Is a Pipedream," *Times of Israel*, March 4, 2018, https://www.timesofisrael.com/in-west-bank-reality-annexation-is-a-pipedream/.

xxxvii Omer Yaniv, Netta Haddad, and Yair Assaf-Shapira, "Jerusalem: Facts and Trends 2022," Jerusalem Institute for Policy Research Publication no. 586, 2022, 18, https://jerusaleminstitute.org.il/wp-content/uploads/2022/05/2022-1-דיגיטל-אנגלית-נתונייך-על.pdf.

xxxviii Meirav Arlosoroff, "Israel's Population Is Growing at a Dizzying Rate. Is It Up for the Challenge?," *Haaretz, January 4, 2021,* https://www.haaretz.com/israel-news/2021-01-04/ty-article-magazine/.premium/israels-population-is-growing-at-a-dizzying-rate-is-it-up-for-the-challenge/0000017f-ef2c-dc28-a17f-ff3f847c0000; and Khaled Abu Toameh, "'Number of Jews and Palestinians Will Be Equal at End of 2022,'" *The Jerusalem Post*, December 31, 2020, https://www.jpost.com/arab-israeli-conflict/number-of-jews-and-palestinians-will-be-equal-at-end-of-2022-653884.

xxxix Yaniv, Haddad, and Assaf-Shapira, 18.

xl Donald J. Trump, "Statement by President Trump on Jerusalem," December 6, 2017, https://trumpwhitehouse.archives.gov/briefings-state ments/statement-president-trump-jerusalem/.

xli Tovah Lazaroff, "Bennett: Area C of West Bank Belongs to Us, We're Waging a Battle for it," *Jerusalem Post*, January 8, 2020, https://www. jpost.com/israel-news/bennett-gov-policy-is-that-area-c-belongs-to-israel-613543.

xlii Jodi Rudoren, "Palestinian Leader Seeks NATO Force in Future State," *The New York Times*, February 2, 2014, https://www.nytimes. com/2014/02/03/world/middleeast/palestinian-leader-seeks-nato-force-in-future-state.html.

xliii Archie Bland, "The Numbers That Reveal the Extent of the Destruction in Gaza," *The Guardian*, January 8, 2024, https://www.theguardian.com/world/2024/jan/08/the-numbers-that-reveal-the-extent-of-the-destruction-in-gaza.

xliv Aya Batrawy, "Gaza's death toll now exceeds 30,000. Here's why it's an incomplete count," *NPR*, February 29, 2024, https://www.npr. org/2024/02/29/1234159514/gaza-death-toll-30000-palestinians-is rael-hamas-war.

xlv See Data on casualties, Office for the Coordination of Humanitarian Affairs, accessed October 24, 2023, https://www.ochaopt.org/data/casualties.

xlvi David K. Shipler, *Arab and Jew: Wounded Spirits in a Promised Land* (New York: Crown, 2015), 221.

xlvii Andrew Higgins, "How Israel Helped to Spawn Hamas," *The Wall Street Journal*, January 24, 2009, http://web.archive.org/web/2009092 6212507/http:/online.wsj.com/article/SB123275572295011847. html.

xlviii Gershom Gorenberg, "Netanyahu Led Us to Catastrophe. He Must Go." *The New York Times*, October 18, 2023, https://www.nytimes. com/2023/10/18/opinion/netanyahu-israel-gaza.html.

xlix Ibid.

l "Gaza Tunnels Stretch at Least 350 Miles, Far Longer than Past Estimate – Report," *Times of Israel*, January 16, 2024, https://www.timesofisrael.com/gaza-tunnels-stretch-at-least-350-miles-far-longer-than-past-estimate-report/.

li Ibid.

lii Adam Raz, "A Brief History of the Netanyahu-Hamas Alliance," *Haaretz*, October 20, 2023, https://www.haaretz.com/israel-news/2023-10-20/ty-article-opinion/.premium/a-brief-history-of-the-netanyahu-hamas-alliance/0000018b-47d9-d242-abef-57ff1be90000.

liii Ibid.

liv "Egypt Intelligence Official Says Israel Ignored Repeated Warnings of 'Something Big,'" *Times of Israel*, October 9, 2023, https://www.timesofisrael.com/egypt-intelligence-official-says-israel-ignored-repeated-warnings-of-something-big/.

lv Nadeen Ebrahim and Vasco Cotovio, "Israeli Government Divisions Deepen as Cabinet Minister Says Defeating Hamas Is Unrealistic," *CNN*, January 20, 2024, https://www.cnn.com/2024/01/19/middleeast/eisenkot-netanyahu-israel-war-politics-gaza-intl/index.html.

lvi Benedict Vigers, "Life in Israel after Oct. 7 in 5 Charts," Gallup, December 22, 2023, https://news.gallup.com/poll/547760/life-israel-oct-charts.aspx.

lvii Jonathan Lis, "New Poll Suggests Israelis Open to Biden Plan Linking Palestinian State to Freeing Hostages, Saudi Normalization," *Haaretz*, January 22, 2024, https://www.haaretz.com/israel-news/2024-01-22/ty-article/.premium/poll-israelis-open-to-biden-plan-linking-palestinian-state-hostages-saudi-normalization/0000018d-3035-dd75-addd-f2f577900000.

lviii Moshe Cohen, "Netanyahu's Likud Continues to Fall below Gantz's National Unity - Poll," *The Jerusalem Post*, January 19, 2024, https://www.jpost.com/israel-news/politics-and-diplomacy/article-782863.

lix Ibid.

lx Gili Cohen, "Ex-Mossad Chief Says Occupation Is Israel's Only Existential Threat," *Haaretz*, March 22, 2017, https://www.haaretz.com/israel-news/2017-03-22/ty-article/ex-mossad-chief-says-occupation-is-israels-only-existential-threat/0000017f-e090-d75c-a7ff-fc9d96a40000.

lxi Jo-Ann Mort, "Meet the Knesset Member Who Revived the Two-State Solution," *The New Republic*, November 14, 2023, https://newrepublic.com/article/176867/meet-knesset-member-revived-two-state-solution.

lxii Sam Sokol and JTA, "Majority of Israelis Oppose Annexation, Resettlement of Gaza – Poll," *Times of Israel*, December 17, 2023, https://www.timesofisrael.com/majority-of-israelis-oppose-annexation-resettlement-of-gaza-poll/.

lxiii Oliver Holmes and Peter Beaumont, "'The Most Popular Palestinian Leader Alive': Releasing Marwan Barghouti Could Transform Territories' Politics," *The Guardian*, February 17, 2024, https://www.theguardian.com/world/2024/feb/17/the-most-popular-palestinian-leader-alive-releasing-marwan-barghouti-could-transform-territories-politics.

lxiv Batrawy.

lxv Matt Shuham, "Benjamin Netanyahu Brags He's 'Proud' To Have Prevented A Palestinian State," *HuffPost*, December 18, 2023, https://www.huffpost.com/entry/benjamin-netanyahu-prevented-palestinian-state-two-state-solution_n_6580a368e4b0e142c0bed60b.

lxvi *The World Factbook 2021*, Washington, D.C.: Central Intelligence Agency, 2021.

lxvii Kathy Gilsinan, "Countries Without Militaries," *The Atlantic*, November 11, 2014, https://www.theatlantic.com/international/archive/2014/11/countries-without-militaries/382606/.

lxviii Patrick Wintour, "Hamas Presents New Charter Accepting a Palestine Based on 1967 Borders," *The Guardian*, May 1, 2017, https://www.theguardian.com/world/2017/may/01/hamas-new-charter-palestine-israel-1967-borders.

lxix "Saudi crown prince says Israelis have right to their own land," *Reuters*,

April 2, 2018, https://www.reuters.com/article/us-saudi-prince-israel /saudi-crown-prince-says-israelis-have-right-to-their-own-land idUSKCN1H91SQ.

lxx Ibid.

lxxi Vivian Salama, "'An open secret': Saudi Arabia and Israel get cozy," *NBC News*, November 15, 2017, https://www.nbcnews.com/news/ mideast/open-secret-saudi-arabia-israel-get-cozy-n821136.

lxxii Gregory Aftandilian, "Jordan and Trump's Peace Plan," Arab Center, Washington, D.C., March 24, 2020, https://arabcenterdc.org/re-source/jordan-and-trumps-peace-plan/.

lxxiii Aaron Magid, "Israel and Jordan's Relationship Is Better Than It Looks," *Foreign Policy*, July 29, 2021, https://foreignpolicy.com/2021 /07/29/israel-jordan-palestine-bennett-netanyahu-abdullah-cold-pe ace/.

lxxiv Yitzhak Gal and Bader Rock, "Israeli-Jordanian Trade: In-Depth Analysis," Tony Blair Institute for Global Change (TBI), October 17, 2018, https://www.institute.global/insights/geopolitics-and-security /israeli-jordanian-trade-depth-analysis.

lxxv Zofeen Ebrahim, "Israel, Jordan, and Palestine Pledge to Clean up Jordan River," *The Third Pole*, August 11, 2015, https://www.thethirdpole. net/en/regional-cooperation/clean-up-jordan-river/.

lxxvi "Egypt's Muslim Brotherhood Declared 'Terrorist Group,'" *BBC News*, December 25, 2013, https://www.bbc.com/news/world-mid dle-east-25515932.

lxxvii "Egypt Court Overturns Hamas Terror Blacklisting," *BBC News*, June 6, 2015, https://www.bbc.com/news/world-middle-east-33034249.

lxxviii "Egypt's foreign minister meets Israeli counterpart in Brussels," *Reuters*, July 11, 2021, https://www.reuters.com/world/middle-east/ egypts-foreign-minister-meets-israeli-counterpart-brussels-2021-0 7-11/.

lxxix KC Johnson, "Why Democrats Are Abandoning Israel," *The Washington Post*, August 18, 2017, https://www.washingtonpost.com/news/ made-by-history/wp/2017/08/18/why-democrats-have-soured-on-israel/.

lxxx Jeremy Sharon and TOI Staff, "Pointing to Hamas's 'Little State,' Netanyahu Touts His Role Blocking 2-State Solution," *Times of Israel*, December 17, 2023, https://www.timesofisrael.com/pointing-to-hamass-little-state-netanyahu-touts-role-blocking-2-state-solution/.

lxxxi Yardena Schwartz, "The Two-School Solution," *Foreign Policy*, May 18, 2016, https://foreignpolicy.com/2016/05/18/the-two-school-soluti on-israeli-arab-children-education-integration/.

lxxxii Nidal Al-Mughrabi, "Hamas Plans More "Enemy Language" Hebrew in Gaza schools," *Reuters*, January 30, 2013, https://www.reuters.com/article/us-palestinians-israel-hebrew/hamas-plans-more-enemy-lan guage-hebrew-in-gaza-schools-idUSBRE90U02C20130131.

lxxxiii Jacob Magid, "11 Months After Announcement, Israeli Building Permits for Palestinians Stalled," *Times of Israel*, June 24, 2020, https://www.timesofisrael.com/11-months-after-announcement-israeli-build ing-permits-for-palestinians-stalled/.

lxxxiv "More than 25,000 Women and Children Killed in Gaza: US Defence Secretary," *Al Jazeera*, March 1, 2024, https://www.aljazeera.com/news/2024/3/1/more-than-25000-women-and-children-killed-in-gaza-us-defence-secretary.

lxxxv Mohammed Haddad and Mohammed Hussein, producers, "Know Their Names: Palestinian Children Killed in Israeli Attacks on Gaza," *Al Jazeera*, January 25, 2024, https://interactive.aljazeera.com/aje/2024/israel-war-on-gaza-10000-children-killed/.

References

"30 Years after Oslo – the Data That Shows How the Settlements Proliferated Following the Oslo Accords." Peace Now, September 11, 2023. https://peacenow.org.il/en/30-years-after-oslo-the-data-that-shows-how-the-settlements-proliferated-following-the-oslo-accords.

Abu Toameh, Khaled. "'Number of Jews and Palestinians Will Be Equal at End of 2022.'" *The Jerusalem Post*, December 31, 2020. https://www.jpost.com/arab-israeli-conflict/number-of-jews-and-palestinians-will-be-equal-at-end-of-2022-653884.

Aftandilian, Gregory. "Jordan and Trump's Peace Plan." Arab Center, Washington, D.C., March 24, 2020. https://arabcenterdc.org/resource/jordan-and-trumps-peace-plan/.

Al Lawati, Abbas, and Nadeen Ebrahim. "Israel Is at War with Hamas. Here's What to Know." *CNN*, October 15, 2023. https://www.cnn.com/2023/10/09/middleeast/israel-hamas-gaza-war-explained-mime-intl/index.html.

Al-Mughrabi, Nidal. "As Gaza Death Toll Rises, Bodies Are Stored in Ice Cream Trucks." *Reuters*, October 15, 2023. https://www.reuters.com/world/middle-east/gaza-death-toll-rises-bodies-are-stored-ice-cream-trucks-2023-10-15/.

Al-Mughrabi, Nidal. "Hamas Plans More "Enemy Language" Hebrew in Gaza Schools." *Reuters*, January 30, 2013. https://www.reuters.com/article/us-palestinians-israel-hebrew/hamas-plans-more-enemy-language-hebrew-in-gaza-schools-idUSBRE90U02C20130131.

Arieli, Shaul, and Nimrod Novik. "In West Bank Reality, Annexation Is a Pipedream." *Times of Israel*, March 4, 2018. https://www.timesofisrael.com/in-west-bank-reality-annexation-is-a-pipedream/.

Arlosoroff, Meirav. "Israel's Population Is Growing at a Dizzying Rate. Is It Up for the Challenge?" *Haaretz*, January 4, 2021. https://www.haaretz.com/israel-news/2021-01-04/ty-article-magazine/.premium/israels-population-is-growing-at-a-dizzying-rate-is-it-up-for-the-challenge/0000017f-ef2c-dc28-a17f-ff3f847c0000.

Ayyub, Rami. "Israeli Minister's Call to 'erase' Palestinian Village an Incitement to Violence, US Says." *Reuters*, March 1, 2023. https://www.reuters.com/world/middle-east/israeli-ministers-call-erase-palestinian-village-an-incitement-violence-us-says-2023-03-01/.

Badiou, Alain. *Polemics*. Translated by Steve Corcoran. New York: Verso, 2012.

Batrawy, Aya. "Gaza's death toll now exceeds 30,000. Here's why it's an incomplete count." *NPR*, February 29, 2024. https://www.npr.org/2024/02/29/1234159514/gaza-death-toll-30000-palestinians-israel-hamas-war.

Ben-Meir, Alon. "The Creation of a Palestinian State is Inescapable." *Jerusalem Post*, June 26, 2021. https://www.jpost.com/opinion/the-creation-of-a-palestinian-state-is-inescapable-opinion-672112.

Ben-Meir, Alon. "Introduction to the Special Issue: Continued Israeli Occupation Is a Ticking Time Bomb." *World Affairs* 185, no. 4 (October 3, 2022): 650-75. https://doi.org/10.1177/00438200221128788.

Ben-Meir, Alon. "Does Israel's Right Cultivate a Permanent Enemy to Justify a Permanent Occupation?" *History News Network*, April 17, 2022. https://historynewsnetwork.org/article/182980.

Ben-Meir, Alon. "Israel-Hamas War Affirms the Indispensability of a Two-State Solution." *Pressenza*, December 6, 2023. https://www.pressenza.com/2023/12/israel-hamas-war-affirms-the-indispensability-of-a-two-state-solution/.

Ben-Meir, Alon. "Now is the Time to Recognize Palestinian Statehood – Opinion." *Jerusalem Post*, January 23, 2024. https://www.jpost.com/opinion/article-783256.

Ben-Meir, Alon. "رأي.. لماذا يعتبر حل الدولتين الخيار الوحيد القابل للتطبيق؟" *CNN*, December 26, 2023. https://arabic.cnn.com/middleeast/article/2023/12/26/two-states-solution-oped-alon-ben-meir.

Ben-Meir, Alon. "The Case for an Israeli-Palestinian-Jordanian Confederation: Why Now and How?" *World Affairs* 185, no. 1 (February 10, 2022): 9-58. https://doi.org/10.1177/00438200211066350.

Ben-Meir, Alon. "Why the Two-State Solution Is the Only Viable Option to the Exclusion of Any Other." *Pressenza*, January 12, 2024. https://www.pressenza.com/2024/01/why-the-two-state-solution-is-the-only-viable-option-to-the-exclusion-of-any-other/.

"Ben-Zvi Sees Population Exchange as Solution of Arab Refugee Problem." Jewish Telegraphic Agency. December 5, 1960. https://www.jta.org/archive/ben-zvi-sees-population-exchange-as-solution-of-arab-refugee-problem.

Bernstein, J.M. "The Harm of Rape, the Harm of Torture." In *Torture and Dignity: An Essay on Moral Injury*, 116-172. Chicago, IL: Chicago University Press, 2015. https://doi.org/10.7208/chicago/9780226266466.003.0004 (accessed October 4, 2022).

Bland, Archie. "The Numbers That Reveal the Extent of the Destruction in Gaza." *The Guardian*, January 8, 2024. https://www.theguardian.com/world/2024/jan/08/the-numbers-that-reveal-the-extent-of-the-destruction-in-gaza.

Breitman, Kendall. "Netanyahu: No Palestinian State on My Watch." *Politico*. March 16, 2015. https://www.politico.com/story/2015/03/benjamin-netanyahu-palestine-116103.

Cohen, Gili. "Ex-Mossad Chief Says Occupation Is Israel's Only Existential Threat." *Haaretz*, March 22, 2017. https://www.haaretz.com/israel-news/2017-03-22/ty-article/ex-mossad-chief-says-occupation-is-israels-only-existential-threat/0000017f-e090-d75c-a7ff-fc9d96a40000.

Cohen, Moshe. "Netanyahu's Likud Continues to Fall below Gantz's National Unity - Poll." *The Jerusalem Post*, January 19, 2024. https://www.jpost.com/israel-news/politics-and-diplomacy/article-782863.

Data on casualties. Accessed October 24, 2023. https://www.ochaopt.org/data/casualties.

"Despite EU Vow to End Incitement, Palestinian Textbooks Remain Unaltered – Report." *The Times of Israel*, January 30, 2022. https://www.timesofisrael.com/despite-eu-vow-to-end-incitement-palestinian-textbooks-remain-unaltered-report/.

Eagleton, Terry. *Ideology*. London: Verso, 1991.

Ebrahim, Nadeen, and Vasco Cotovio. "Israeli Government Divisions Deepen as Cabinet Minister Says Defeating Hamas Is Unrealistic." *CNN*, January 20, 2024. https://www.cnn.com/2024/01/19/middleeast/eisenkot-netanyahu-israel-war-politics-gaza-intl/index.html.

Ebrahim, Zofeen. "Israel, Jordan and Palestine Pledge to Clean up Jordan River." *The Third Pole*, August 11, 2015. https://www.

thethirdpole.net/en/regional-cooperation/clean-up-jordan-river/.

"Egypt Court Overturns Hamas Terror Blacklisting." *BBC News*, June 6, 2015. https://www.bbc.com/news/world-middle-east-33034249.

"Egypt Intelligence Official Says Israel Ignored Repeated Warnings of 'Something Big.'" *Times of Israel*, October 9, 2023. https://www.timesofisrael.com/egypt-intelligence-official-says-israel-ignored-repeated-warnings-of-something-big/.

"Egypt's Foreign Minister Meets Israeli Counterpart in Brussels." *Reuters*, July 11, 2021. https://www.reuters.com/world/middle-east/egypts-foreign-minister-meets-israeli-counterpart-brussels-2021-07-11/.

"Egypt's Muslim Brotherhood Declared 'Terrorist Group.'" *BBC News*, December 25, 2013. https://www.bbc.com/news/world-middle-east-25515932.

Freud, Sigmund. *The Future of an Illusion*. Translated by Gregory C. Richter, edited by Todd Dufresne. Peterborough: Broadview Press, 2012.

Gal, Yitzhak, and Bader Rock. "Israeli-Jordanian Trade: In-Depth Analysis." Tony Blair Institute for Global Change (TBI), October 17, 2018. https://www.institute.global/insights/geopolitics-and-security/israeli-jordanian-trade-depth-analysis.

"Gaza Strip: Acute Food Insecurity Situation for 24 November - 7 December 2023 and Projection for 8 December 2023 - 7 February 2024." IPC Portal, December 21, 2023. https://www.ipcinfo.org/ipc-country-analysis/details-map/en/c/1156749/?iso3=PSE.

"Gaza Tunnels Stretch at Least 350 Miles, Far Longer than Past Es-

timate – Report." *The Times of Israel,* January 16, 2024. https://
www.timesofisrael.com/gaza-tunnels-stretch-at-least-350-
miles-far-longer-than-past-estimate-report/.

General Assembly Agenda Item 10, Declaration of Principles on
Interim Self-Government Arrangements, A/48/486 (11 October 1993), available from https://peacemaker.un.org/israel
opt-osloaccord93.

Gilsinan, Kathy. "Countries Without Militaries." *The Atlantic,* November 11, 2014. https://www.theatlantic.com/international
/archive/2014/11/countries-without-militaries/382606/.

Gorenberg, Gershom. "Netanyahu Led Us to Catastrophe. He
Must Go." *The New York Times,* October 18, 2023. https://
www.nytimes.com/2023/10/18/opinion/netanyahu-israel-
gaza.html.

Gramlich, John. "What the data says about gun deaths in the U.S."
Pew Research Center, April 26, 2023. https://www.pewre
search.org/short-reads/2023/04/26/what-the-data-says-
about-gun-deaths-in-the-u-s/.

Haberman, Clyde. "Shamir Is Said to Admit Plan to Stall Talks 'for
10 Years.'" *The New York Times,* June 27, 1992. https://www.
nytimes.com/1992/06/27/world/shamir-is-said-to-admit-
plan-to-stall-talks-for-10-years.html.

Haddad, Mohammed, and Mohammed Hussein, producers.
"Know Their Names: Palestinian Children Killed in Israeli Attacks on Gaza." *Al Jazeera,* January 25, 2024. https://interac
tive.aljazeera.com/aje/2024/israel-war-on-gaza-10000-chil
dren-killed/.

Higgins, Andrew. "How Israel Helped to Spawn Hamas." *The
Wall Street Journal,* January 24, 2009. http://web.archive.org/

web/20090926212507/http:/online.wsj.com/article/
SB123275572295011847.html.

Hoffman, Gil and Tovah Lazaroff. "No Palestinian State under
Bennett-Led Government, FM Says." *The Jerusalem Post*, August
20, 2021. https://www.jpost.com/israel-news/no-palestinian-
state-under-bennett-led-government-lapid-says-677235.

Holmes, Oliver, and Peter Beaumont. "'The Most Popular Palestinian Leader Alive': Releasing Marwan Barghouti Could
Transform Territories' Politics." *The Guardian*, February 17,
2024. https://www.theguardian.com/world/2024/feb/17/
the-most-popular-palestinian-leader-alive-releasing-mar
wan-barghouti-could-transform-territories-politics.

"ISA Detains and Interrogates B'Tselem Field Researcher; B'Tselem: 'Disgraceful Arrest Aimed at Hampering the Work of a
Human Rights Organization.'" B'Tselem, August 12, 2022.
https://www.btselem.org/press_releases/20220812_isa_de
tains_and_interrogates_btselem_field_researcher.

Jefferis, Jennifer. *Hamas: Terrorism, Governance, and Its Future in
Middle East Politics*. Santa Barbara, CA: Praeger, 2016.

Joffe, Alexander, and Asaf Romirowsky. "The Politics of the Palestinian Right of Return." *Forbes*, February 24, 2014. https://www.forbes.com/sites/realspin/2014/02/24/the-poli
tics-of-the-palestinian-right-of-return/?sh=5eaab30c608b.

Johnson, KC. "Why Democrats Are Abandoning Israel." *The Washington Post*, August 18, 2017. https://www.washingtonpost.
com/news/made-by-history/wp/2017/08/18/why-demo
crats-have-soured-on-israel/.

Kampeas, Ron. "Bennett: Israel won't Annex Territory or Establish
Palestinian State on My Watch." *Times of Israel*, August 25, 2021.

https://www.timesofisrael.com/bennett-israel-wont-annex-territory-or-establish-palestinian-state-on-my-watch/.

Kashti, Or. "In Israeli Textbooks, the Palestinians Are All But Invisible." *Haaretz*, June 21, 2020. https://www.haaretz.com/israel-news/2020-06-21/ty-article/.premium/in-israeli-textbooks-the-palestinians-are-all-but-invisible/0000017f-f53a-d318-afff-f77b47ba0000.

Kelman, Herbert C. "The Social Context of Torture: Policy Process and Authority Structure." In *The Politics of Pain: Torturers and Their Masters*, 19-34. New York: Routledge, 2019.

Kershner, Isabel. "Palestinian Leader Accused Israel of '50 Holocausts,' Causing an Uproar." *The New York Times*, August 17, 2022. https://www.nytimes.com/2022/08/17/world/middleeast/palestinian-leader-accused-israel-of-50-holocausts-causing-an-uproar.html.

Korach, Michal, and Maya Chosen. "Jerusalem Facts and Trends." Jerusalem Institute for Policy Research. Publication no. 485. 2018. https://jerusaleminstitute.org.il/wp-content/uploads/2019/06/PUB_%D7%A2%D7%9C-%D7%A0%D7%AA%D7%95%D7%A0%D7%99%D7%99%D7%9A-%D7%90%D7%A0%D7%92%D7%9C%D7%99%D7%AA-2018-%D7%93%D7%99%D7%92%D7%99%D7%98%D7%9C-%D7%A1-%D7%95%D7%A4%D7%99_eng.pdf.

Lasensky, Scott B. "How to Help Palestinian Refugees Today." Jerusalem Center for Public Affairs, February 2, 2003. https://www.jcpa.org/jl/vp491.htm.

Lazaroff, Tovah. "Bennett: Area C of West Bank Belongs to Us, We're Waging a Battle for it." *Jerusalem Post*, January 8, 2020. https://www.jpost.com/israel-news/bennett-gov-policy-is-that-area-c-belongs-to-israel-613543.

"Likud Party Platform from the 15th Knesset." Webarchive.org. 1999, accessed October 5, 2022. https://web.archive.org/web /20070930181442/https://www.knesset.gov.il/elections/ knesset15/elikud_m.htm.

Lis, Jonathan. "New Poll Suggests Israelis Open to Biden Plan Linking Palestinian State to Freeing Hostages, Saudi Normalization." *Haaretz*, January 22, 2024. https://www.haaretz.com/ israel-news/2024-01-22/ty-article/.premium/poll-israelis-open-to-biden-plan-linking-palestinian-state-hostages-saudi-normalization/0000018d-3035-dd75-addd-f2f577900000.

Magid, Aaron. "Israel and Jordan's Relationship Is Better Than It Looks." *Foreign Policy*, July 29, 2021. https://foreignpolicy. com/2021/07/29/israel-jordan-palestine-bennett-netanya hu-abdullah-cold-peace/.

Magid, Jacob. "11 Months After Announcement, Israeli Building Permits for Palestinians Stalled." *Times of Israel*, June 24, 2020. https://www.timesofisrael.com/11-months-after-announce ment-israeli-building-permits-for-palestinians-stalled/.

McLaughlin, Eliott C. "Israel's PM Netanyahu: No Palestinian state on my watch." *CNN*, March 16, 2015. https://www. cnn.com/2015/03/16/middleeast/israel-netanyahu-palestin ian-state/index.html.

"More than 100 Palestinians Killed in West Bank amid Gaza War." *France 24*, October 25, 2023. https://www.france24.com/en/ live-news/20231025-more-than-100-palestinians-killed-in-west-bank-amid-gaza-war.

"More than 25,000 Women and Children Killed in Gaza: US Defence Secretary." *Al Jazeera*, March 1, 2024. https://www.alja zeera.com/news/2024/3/1/more-than-25000-women-and-children-killed-in-gaza-us-defence-secretary.

Mort, Jo-Ann. "Meet the Knesset Member Who Revived the Two-State Solution." *The New Republic*, November 14, 2023. https://newrepublic.com/article/176867/meet-knesset-member-revived-two-state-solution.

Netanyahu, Benjamin. "Text of PM Binyamin Netanyahu's speech to the US Congress." *Jerusalem Post*, May 24, 2011, accessed October 1, 2022. http://www.jpost.com/DiplomacyAndPolitics/Article.aspx?id=222056.

Palestinian Bureau of Central Statistics. "On the occasion of the International Youth Day, the Palestinian Central Bureau of Statistics (PCBS) issues a press release demonstrating the situation of youth in the Palestinian society." December 8, 2020. https://www.pcbs.gov.ps/site/512/default.aspx?lang=en&ItemID=3787.

"Poll Summary: Palestinian-Israeli Pulse." Palestinian Center for Policy and Survey Research, August 13, 2018. https://www.pcpsr.org/en/node/731.

Rabinowitz, David. "The Psychological Dimensions of the Israeli-Palestinian Conflict: The Role of Psychological Resistance." In correspondence with the author, Haifa, Israel, 2012.

Raz, Adam. "A Brief History of the Netanyahu-Hamas Alliance." *Haaretz*, October 20, 2023. https://www.haaretz.com/israel-news/2023-10-20/ty-article-opinion/.premium/a-brief-history-of-the-netanyahu-hamas-alliance/0000018b-47d9-d242-abef-57ff1be90000.

"Results of PSR Refugees' Polls in the West Bank/Gaza Strip, Jordan and Lebanon on Refugees' Preferences and Behavior in a Palestinian-Israeli Permanent Refugee Agreement." Palestinian Center for Policy and Survey Research. January-June 2003. https://www.pcpsr.org/en/node/493.

Rudoren, Jodi. "Palestinian Leader Seeks NATO Force in Future State." *The New York Times*, February 2, 2014. https://www.nytimes.com/2014/02/03/world/middleeast/palestinian-leader-seeks-nato-force-in-future-state.html.

Salama, Vivian. "'An open secret': Saudi Arabia and Israel get cozy." *NBC News*, November 15, 2017. https://www.nbcnews.com/news/mideast/open-secret-saudi-arabia-israel-get-cozy-n821136.

"Saudi crown prince says Israelis have right to their own land." *Reuters*, April 2, 2018. https://www.reuters.com/article/us-saudi-prince-israel/saudi-crown-prince-says-israelis-have-right-to-their-own-land-idUSKCN1H91SQ.

Schwartz, Yardena. "The Two-School Solution." *Foreign Policy*, May 18, 2016. https://foreignpolicy.com/2016/05/18/the-two-school-solution-israeli-arab-children-education-integration/.

Shakir, Omar. "Raising the Alarm: Israel's All-Out Assault on Rights Defenders." Human Rights Watch, August 19, 2022. https://www.hrw.org/news/2022/08/19/raising-alarm-israels-all-out-assault-rights-defenders.

Sharon, Jeremy, and TOI Staff. "Pointing to Hamas's 'Little State,' Netanyahu Touts His Role Blocking 2-State Solution." *Times of Israel*, December 17, 2023. https://www.timesofisrael.com/pointing-to-hamass-little-state-netanyahu-touts-role-blocking-2-state-solution/.

Shenhav, Yehouda. "Arab Jews, Population Exchange, and the Palestinian Right of Return." In *Exile and Return: Predicaments of Palestinians and Jews*, edited by Ann M. Lesch and Ian S. Lustick, 225-245. Philadelphia: University of Pennsylvania Press, 2008.

Shipler, David K. *Arab and Jew: Wounded Spirits in a Promised Land.* New York: Crown, 2015.

Shuham, Matt. "Benjamin Netanyahu Brags He's 'Proud' To Have Prevented a Palestinian State." *HuffPost,* December 18, 2023. https://www.huffpost.com/entry/benjamin-netanyahu-prevented-palestinian-state-two-state-solution_n_6580a368e4b0e142c0bed60b.

Sokol, Sam, and JTA. "Majority of Israelis Oppose Annexation, Resettlement of Gaza – Poll." *Times of Israel,* December 17, 2023. https://www.timesofisrael.com/majority-of-israelis-oppose-annexation-resettlement-of-gaza-poll/.

Sullivan, Becky. "Israel Incursion into Gaza Targeted Hamas Leaders to Prepare for 'next Stages of War.'" *NPR,* October 26, 2023. https://www.npr.org/2023/10/26/1208680784/death-toll-in-gaza-approaches-7-000-as-aid-groups-raise-alarm-about-fuel.

"Terminology." United Nations Peacekeeping. Accessed February 23, 2024. https://peacekeeping.un.org/en/terminology.

"The Covenant of the Islamic Resistance Movement." The Avalon Project, August 18, 1988 (accessed October 1, 2022). http://avalon.law.yale.edu/20th_century/hamas.asp.

"The Situation of Workers of the Occupied Arab Territories." International Labour Organization. 2020. https://www.ilo.org/wcmsp5/groups/public/---ed_norm/---relconf/documents/meetingdocument/wcms_745966.pdf.

The World Factbook 2021. Washington, D.C.: Central Intelligence Agency, 2021.

Trump, Donald J. "Statement by President Trump on Jerusalem." December 6, 2017. https://trumpwhitehouse.archives.gov/

briefings-statements/statement-president-trump-jerusalem/.

Tuastad, Dag Henrik. "The Hudna: Hamas's Concept of a Long-term Ceasefire." PRIO Policy Brief, 9. Oslo: PRIO, 2010. https://www.prio.org/publications/7356.

United Nations. "Khartoum Resolution." September 1, 1967, accessed October 2, 2022. https://www.un.org/unispal/docum ent/auto-insert-193039/.

United States Department of State. "Secretary Blinken's Call with Israeli Prime Minister Netanyahu." May 12, 2021. https://www. state.gov/secretary-blinkens-call-with-israeli-prime-minis ter-netanyahu/.

UNRWA. "Palestine Refugees." United Nations Relief and Works Agency, accessed September 1, 2022. https://www.unrwa. org/palestine-refugees.

Vigers, Benedict. "Life in Israel after Oct. 7 in 5 Charts." Gallup, December 22, 2023. https://news.gallup.com/poll/547760/ life-israel-oct-charts.aspx.

"What Are Area A, Area B, and Area C in the West Bank?" Anera, September 21, 2023. https://www.anera.org/what-are-area-a-area-b-and-area-c-in-the-west-bank/.

"Why the Palestinian Group Hamas Launched an Attack on Israel? All to Know." *Al Jazeera*, October 9, 2023. https://www. aljazeera.com/news/2023/10/7/palestinian-group-hamas-launches-surprise-attack-on-israel-what-to-know.

Wintour, Patrick. "Hamas Presents New Charter Accepting a Palestine Based on 1967 Borders." *The Guardian*, May 1, 2017. https://www.theguardian.com/world/2017/may/01/hamas -new-charter-palestine-israel-1967-borders.

Yaniv, Omer, Netta Haddad, and Yair Assaf-Shapira. "Jerusalem: Facts and Trends 2022." Jerusalem Institute for Policy Research Publication no. 586, 2022. https://jerusaleminstitute.org.il/wp-content/uploads/2022/05/2022--עַל-נתונייך אנגלית-דיגיטל-1.pdf.

Yeung, Jessie, Kareem El Damanhoury, Eyad Kourdi, Niamh Kennedy, Sophie Jeong, Abeer Salman, and Sophie Tanno. "Israel Warns of New Phase in War on Hamas, as Gaza Civilians Flee and Israeli Troops Gather near Border." *CNN*, October 14, 2023. https://www.cnn.com/2023/10/14/middleeast/gaza-israel-evacuation-saturday-intl-hnk/index.html.

Dr. Alon Ben Meir is a retired professor of international affairs, most recently having taught at New York University's Center for Global Affairs. Ben-Meir is an expert on Middle East and West Balkan affairs, international negotiations, and conflict resolution. In the past two decades, Ben-Meir has been directly involved in various backchannel negotiations involving Israel and its neighboring countries and Turkey.

Ben-Meir is featured on a variety of television networks and also regularly briefs at the U.S. State Department for the International Visitors Program. He writes a weekly article that is syndicated globally.

Dr. Ben-Meir has authored seven books related to the Middle East and is currently working on a new book that expands upon his proposal for an Israeli-Palestinian-Jordanian Confederation. Ben-Meir holds a master's degree in philosophy and a doctorate in international relations from Oxford University.

Related Titles from Westphalia Press

The Limits of Moderation: Jimmy Carter and the Ironies of American Liberalism

The Limits of Moderation: Jimmy Carter and the Ironies of American Liberalism is not a finished product. And yet, even in this unfinished stage, this book is a close and careful history of a short yet transformative period in American political history, when big changes were afoot.

The Zelensky Method
by Grant Farred

Locating Russian's war within a global context, The Zelensky Method is unsparing in its critique of those nations, who have refused to condemn Russia's invasion and are doing everything they can to prevent economic sanctions from being imposed on the Kremlin.

Sinking into the Honey Trap: The Case of the Israeli-Palestinian Conflict
by Daniel Bar-Tal, Barbara Doron, Translator

Sinking into the Honey Trap by Daniel Bar-Tal discusses how politics led Israel to advancing the occupation, and of the deterioration of democracy and morality that accelerates the growth of an authoritarian regime with nationalism and religiosity.

Essay on The Mysteries and the True Object of The Brotherhood of Freemasons
by Jason Williams

The third edition of Essai sur les mystères discusses Freemasonry's role as a society of symbolic philosophers who cultivate their minds, practice virtues, and engage in charity, and underscores the importance of brotherhood, morality, and goodwill.

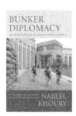

Bunker Diplomacy: An Arab-American in the U.S. Foreign Service
by Nabeel Khoury

After twenty-five years in the Foreign Service, Dr. Nabeel A. Khoury retired from the U.S. Department of State in 2013 with the rank of Minister Counselor. In his last overseas posting, Khoury served as deputy chief of mission at the U.S. embassy in Yemen (2004-2007).

Managing Challenges for the Flint Water Crisis
Edited by Toyna E. Thornton, Andrew D. Williams, Katherine M. Simon, Jennifer F. Sklarew

This edited volume examines several public management and intergovernmental failures, with particular attention on social, political, and financial impacts. Understanding disaster meaning, even causality, is essential to the problem-solving process.

User-Centric Design
by Dr. Diane Stottlemyer

User-centric strategy can improve by using tools to manage performance using specific techniques. User-centric design is based on and centered around the users. They are an essential part of the design process and should have a say in what they want and need from the application based on behavior and performance.

How the Rampant Proliferation of Disinformation Has Become the New Pandemic, and What To Do About It by Max Joseph Skidmore Jr.

This work examines the causes of the overwhelming tidal wave of fake news, misinformation, disinformation, and propaganda, and the increase in information illiteracy and mistrust in higher education and traditional, vetted news outlets that make fact-checking a priority.

Abortion and Informed Common Sense
by Max J. Skidmore

The controversy over a woman's "right to choose," as opposed to the numerous "rights" that abortion opponents decide should be assumed to exist for "unborn children," has always struck me as incomplete. Two missing elements of the argument seems obvious, yet they remain almost completely overlooked.

The Athenian Year Primer: Attic Time-Reckoning and the Julian Calendar
by Christopher Planeaux

The ability to translate ancient Athenian calendar references into precise Julian-Gregorian dates will not only assist Ancient Historians and Classicists to date numerous historical events with much greater accuracy but also aid epigraphists in the restorations of numerous Attic inscriptions.

Siddhartha: Life of the Buddha
by David L. Phillips,
contributions by Venerable Sitagu Sayadaw

Siddhartha: Life of the Buddha is an illustrated story for adults and children about the Buddha's birth, enlightenment and work for social justice. It includes illustrations from Pagan, Burma which are provided by Rev. Sitagu Sayadaw.

Growing Inequality: Bridging Complex Systems, Population Health, and Health Disparities
Editors: George A. Kaplan, Ana V. Diez Roux, Carl P. Simon, and Sandro Galea

Why is America's health is poorer than the health of other wealthy countries and why health inequities persist despite our efforts? In this book, researchers report on groundbreaking insights to simulate how these determinants come together to produce levels of population health and disparities and test new solutions.

Issues in Maritime Cyber Security
Edited by Dr. Joe DiRenzo III, Dr. Nicole K. Drumhiller, and Dr. Fred S. Roberts

The complexity of making MTS safe from cyber attack is daunting and the need for all stakeholders in both government (at all levels) and private industry to be involved in cyber security is more significant than ever as the use of the MTS continues to grow.

Female Emancipation and Masonic Membership: An Essential Collection
By Guillermo De Los Reyes Heredia

Female Emancipation and Masonic Membership: An Essential Combination is a collection of essays on Freemasonry and gender that promotes a transatlantic discussion of the study of the history of women and Freemasonry and their contribution in different countries.

Anti-Poverty Measures in America: Scientism and Other Obstacles
Editors, Max J. Skidmore and Biko Koenig

Anti-Poverty Measures in America brings together a remarkable collection of essays dealing with the inhibiting effects of scientism, an over-dependence on scientific methodology that is prevalent in the social sciences, and other obstacles to anti-poverty legislation.

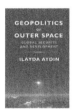

Geopolitics of Outer Space: Global Security and Development
by Ilayda Aydin

A desire for increased security and rapid development is driving nation-states to engage in an intensifying competition for the unique assets of space. This book analyses the Chinese-American space discourse from the lenses of international relations theory, history and political psychology to explore these questions.

Contests of Initiative: Countering China's Gray Zone Strategy in the East and South China Seas
by Dr. Raymond Kuo

China is engaged in a widespread assertion of sovereignty in the South and East China Seas. It employs a "gray zone" strategy: using coercive but sub-conventional military power to drive off challengers and prevent escalation, while simultaneously seizing territory and asserting maritime control.

Discourse of the Inquisitive
Editors: Jaclyn Maria Fowler and Bjorn Mercer

Good communication skills are necessary for articulating learning, especially in online classrooms. It is often through writing that learners demonstrate their ability to analyze and synthesize the new concepts presented in the classroom.

westphaliapress.org

Policy Studies Organization

The Policy Studies Organization (PSO) is a publisher of academic journals and book series, sponsor of conferences, and producer of programs.

Policy Studies Organization publishes dozens of journals on a range of topics, such as European Policy Analysis, Journal of Elder Studies, Indian Politics & Polity, Journal of Critical Infrastructure Policy, and Popular Culture Review.

Additionally, Policy Studies Organization hosts numerous conferences. These conferences include the Middle East Dialogue, Space Education and Strategic Applications Conference, International Criminology Conference, Dupont Summit on Science, Technology and Environmental Policy, World Conference on Fraternalism, Freemasonry and History, and the Internet Policy & Politics Conference.

For more information on these projects, access videos of past events, and upcoming events, please visit us at:

www.ipsonet.org

Made in the USA
Columbia, SC
18 May 2024

35840704R00098